No Evil Shall Befall Thee

No Evil Shall Befall Thee

by
Kennith Stewart, D. Min.

Harrison House
Tulsa, Oklahoma

Unless otherwise indicated, all Scripture quotations are taken from *The Holy Bible, King James Version.*

No Evil Shall Befall Thee
ISBN 0-89274-770-6
Copyright © 1991 by Kennith E. Stewart, D. Min.
P. O. Box 2493
Broken Arrow, Oklahoma 74013-2493

Published by Harrison House, Inc.
P. O. Box 35035
Tulsa, Oklahoma 74153

Contents

Introduction

The protection of God is a pivotal issue in the life of the Church. In fact, there is probably no other singular issue about which there is more confusion in the Church.

On a daily basis we see Christians victimized, abused, and suffering just the same as those who do not know God. Of course, this raises some very serious questions.

Do I have a right as a believer to expect my life to really be any different from the unbeliever's? Spiritually, I know that my life is. But in terms of health, accidents and outright attacks from evil forces, does God really provide any extra benefits to me as His child?

I am shocked and amazed at the variety of answers I have received to those questions. They run to both extremes.

There are those people who speak as though God provides no protection at all for His children. Many people even go as far as to accuse God of doing the very things from which Psalm 91 says He will protect us.

Yet, at the other extreme there are those who seem to believe that God's guardianship is irrevocable. They also seem to have no understanding that there are conditions to be met.

Somewhere in the middle of all the confusion and extremes is the Bible answer we are all longing to discover. A balance on this subject does exist.

While I do not begin to believe that I can explain fully even a small percentage of the calamities that have befallen Christians, I do believe God has given me something to say on the subject. Be assured, I also deplore and reject simplistic answers to vital life and death questions.

I also want to know WHY?

But, I do not know all the whys. I only know that God's Word is true. If we will simply learn to take it for what it says, we will in this lifetime understand enough of those nagging questions.

As you read the following pages, I sincerely hope that two things leap from the page again and again. The first is extremely important. There are always conditions to be met. The second is even more important. God really loves you, and that is why He made all the conditions.

You see, I did not make the conditions I am going to point out to you. This is not a book designed to support a particular religious dogma. Rather, it is my sincere desire to clearly and accurately present truth from God's Word on this vital subject.

At a time when violence, crime, hatred, abuse, fear and anger are on the rise at an unprecedented rate, this subject is most important. I urge you to take this book to heart.

Read it carefully. Meditate on the principles you find here. Allow them to bring strength and courage to your heart. That was God's original intent when He inspired the psalmist with these beautiful words. It is only my humble privilege to make a few comments about what was written in this psalm.

May any blessing these words bring to your life ultimately bring even greater glory and joy to the heart of God.

Psalm 91

He that dwelleth in the secret place of the most High shall abide under the shadow of the Almighty.

I will say of the Lord, He is my refuge and my fortress: my God; in him will I trust.

Surely he shall deliver thee from the snare of the fowler, and from the noisome pestilence.

He shall cover thee with his feathers, and under his wings shalt thou trust: his truth shall be thy shield and buckler.

Thou shalt not be afraid for the terror by night; nor for the arrow that flieth by day;

Nor for the pestilence that walketh in darkness; nor for the destruction that wasteth at noonday.

A thousand shall fall at thy side, and ten thousand at thy right hand; but it shall not come nigh thee.

Only with thine eyes shalt thou behold and see the reward of the wicked.

Because thou hast made the Lord, which is my refuge, even the most High, thy habitation;

There shall no evil befall thee, neither shall any plague come nigh thy dwelling.

For he shall give his angels charge over thee, to keep thee in all thy ways.

They shall bear thee up in their hands, lest thou dash thy foot against a stone.

Thou shalt tread upon the lion and adder: the young lion and the dragon shalt thou trample under foot.

Because he hath set his love upon me, therefore will I deliver him: I will set him on high, because he hath known my name.

He shall call upon me, and I will answer him: I will be with him in trouble; I will deliver him, and honour him.

With long life will I satisfy him, and shew him my salvation.

1
Dwelling in the Secret Place

He that dwelleth in the secret place
of the most High...

Psalm 91:1

Almost all Christians I know believe they should be able to benefit from the things spoken of in Psalm 91. However, a careful reading of it will show clearly that the promises are not *for* everyone.

The 91st Psalm has been called the "serviceman's psalm" because men on the battle front have talked of reciting this in prayer and relying on its promises for protection.

I recall hearing a story about a serviceman who carried a New Testament with the Psalms in his shirt pocket. He was shot in battle, the story goes, and the bullet went through the New Testament and lodged at the seventh verse of the 91st Psalm!

A thousand shall fall at thy side and ten thousand
at thy right hand; but it shall not come nigh thee.

That is a good story, and I like it. However, the story may be true, and it may not. I do not know. I would like to believe it is true, and if so, I would like to meet the man to whom this happened. However, the purpose of this psalm is not for people to carry Bibles in their pockets for protection.

The psalmist did not say, "He who carries a New Testament in his shirt pocket shall abide under the shadow of the Almighty."

9

The psalmist makes it clear who he is talking about: those who dwell in the secret place of God. Everything that follows those words in this psalm applies to those people. Anyone who chooses can make the decision to dwell in the secret place of the Most High.

However, most Christians have not made that decision. Many people are born again. But only a few have made the decision to dwell in God's secret place.

Just because you have confessed that "Jesus Christ is Lord" does not mean you are dwelling in the secret place of the Lord. There is a lot more to this psalm than that — but that is the place to start. Any born-again person can choose to dwell there. You do not have to be rich, nor do you have to be poor; you do not have to be smart, nor do you have to be dumb. You just have to be born again and make a decision to live in God's secret place.

The word *dwell* means "to make one's home; reside; live."[1] *Dwell* refers to your habitat, your environment, where you are from day to day. So anyone who makes the decision that the **secret place of the most High** will be his dwelling place, his residence, his habitat, his home — and who abides by that decision — can begin to claim what is said in the 91st Psalm.

However, being able to live in that secret place requires meeting some conditions.

As a Christian, I must first accept the Bible as being God's words spoken directly to me as an individual. For example, when the Scripture says that God will ...**give his angels charge over thee, to keep thee in all thy ways** (Ps. 91:11), it is necessary to take that very personally. I must believe that God will do that for me. In addition to believing these things, it is necessary also to talk and act as if I believe them. I must come to expect them to happen in my life.

---

[1] *Webster's New World Dictionary*, 3d Coll. Ed., S. V. "dwell."

Another way of expressing the same idea is to refer to it as "abiding in Jesus." In cases such as this, the actual teachings or commandments of Jesus as recorded in the Scriptures are usually being referred to. Again, I must take them very personally, as though Jesus was speaking directly to me. I must obey what Jesus has said. I must expect the things He has spoken to happen in my life.

The Psalm Has Conditions

I have known people who said to their children, friends or family members, "Well, just claim the 91st Psalm. After all, you are a born-again Christian, so just claim what it says there, and God will have to do it."

I have heard that said *so* many times! However, being born again is only the first step. How do you make the decision to dwell in that secret place? Look at Ephesians 3:

> **For this cause I bow my knees unto the Father of our Lord Jesus Christ,**
>
> **Of whom the whole family in heaven and earth is named.**

> **Ephesians 3:14,15**

Notice who that verse is talking about: God's *family*. The first thing that comes to my mind about that verse, in the context of all that I have written above, is people dwelling together, having their habitat together, living in the same household.

The Apostle Paul was writing here about the whole family in heaven and earth that is named after God.

> **That he would grant you, according to the riches of his glory, to be strengthened with might by his Spirit in the inner man;**
>
> **That Christ may dwell in your hearts by faith; that ye, being rooted and grounded in love,**
>
> **May be able to comprehend with all saints what is the breadth, and length, and depth, and height;**

11

> **And to know the love of Christ, which passeth knowledge, that ye might be filled with all the fulness of God.**
>
> **Ephesians 3:16-19**

In these verses, Paul was telling the Ephesians — and all Christians who have lived since his time — how to dwell in the secret place of the Most High. Actually, he was praying. This is the kind of petition Paul was making to the Father:

"I am going to pray for you, and I'm bowing my knees unto the Father of our Lord Jesus Christ. I'm bowing to the Father because it is *in* His name, it is *by* His name, it is *through* His name, it is *with* His name, that the whole family in heaven and in earth is named."

What family does Paul mean? All of those who are born again. So when Paul prayed this prayer, he prayed it not only for the Christians at Ephesus but for all of us that we might be strengthened in the inner man so that Christ may dwell in our hearts by faith.

Paul was praying for those of us who are born again that Jesus might dwell in our hearts by faith, that Jesus might take up residence within us, that He might become a part of each of us in order that we might comprehend the riches of glory in Him. The "riches of His glory" that we may have are spelled out in verses 2-16 of the 91st Psalm.

How To Be Satisfied With Life

I will get ahead of myself a little bit and give you an example of the "length, depth, breadth, and height." The last verse of the 91st Psalm says, **With long life will I satisfy him.** (v. 16.) To some people "long life" is fifty, sixty, or seventy years. To others, it is ninety or a hundred. How about the word *satisfy?*

Are you satisfied with life? Are you 100 percent, absolutely, completely, without a doubt at all, satisfied with life? We do not even begin to comprehend what that means or what it would be like to be satisfied with life, much less satisfied with *long* life.

So we can see that there is something about dwelling in the secret place of the Most High that has to do with Christ dwelling in us richly. I believe the reason we have such a hard time understanding that concept is that we have a hard time receiving a real revelation of the fact that Christ can dwell in our hearts by faith.

In Ephesians 3:17, the Apostle Paul also talked about Christians being "grounded in love." Let us look at that for a moment.

You say to someone, "I love you," and perhaps you do try to show that you love the person. Yet, every now and then, Satan is able to slip in and cause some word to be said or some act to be done that really does not communicate love.

Paul's prayer was that Christ might dwell in Christians' hearts by faith so that they might be rooted and grounded in love. If we are rooted and grounded in the love of Christ, the times when we do not show love to others become farther and farther apart. Every day of our lives, we need to be so rooted and grounded in Christ that we show love toward everyone with whom we come in contact.

Therefore, the way to dwell in the secret place of the Most High is: Number one, be born again; and number two, turn your whole heart over to Christ so that He really does dwell in you. If you walk in love, people can see Jesus in you.

When you make the decision to be born again — to believe in your heart and confess with your mouth that Jesus is Lord (Rom. 10:9,10) — in that moment, the Spirit of God's Son, the Spirit of adoption, moves into your heart.

From that moment forward, the hardest job Jesus has is to keep you from throwing Him out of certain areas of your heart. He wants to make more and more of you His dwelling place. When you confess that Jesus is Lord, and He moves into your heart as Savior, that state should not only continue but progress.

If you have genuinely made that confession, you *are* born again. But you have heard or read about the house that was cleaned, garnished, and left empty, have you not? And because it was cleaned but remained empty, the evil spirit that left came back into the heart and brought seven others worse than he. (Luke 11:24-26.)

This is not written to frighten nor to bring any condemnation on you; however, what I want you to understand is that becoming born again is just the beginning. From that day forward, you are responsible to read God's Word, to pray, and to allow Jesus to fill more and more of your heart by faith so that you can trust Him more and more.

Simply because you confess that Jesus Christ is Lord does not mean that Jesus moves in and lives there from then on. Otherwise, Paul would never have had to pray this prayer for the whole family in heaven and in earth. Being born again is just the introduction that opens the door for Jesus to enter. Then you want to keep Him indwelling your heart.

The psalmist, of course, did not understand this, being born so many hundreds of years before Jesus was crucified and resurrected. We have a New Covenant, and in studying this psalm, we are looking back on the days of the Old Covenant.

As Jesus dwells in your heart, you will begin to understand a lot of things and know more about the love of Christ that passes understanding. You will know more and more about it, but you will never comprehend His love totally — because the Word says His love surpasses our natural knowledge. (Eph. 3:19.)

Dwelling in the secret place of the Most High does not simply involve *your* moving into the Kingdom of God. It also is based on your allowing *the King* to move into your heart. Because the King has moved into your heart, you have a right to live in His Kingdom.

Philippians 3:20 says:

For our conversation is in heaven; from whence also we look for the Saviour, the Lord Jesus Christ:

The Greek word *politeuma* translated *conversation* in the *King James Version* is translated differently in other versions, because *conversation* means something different to us today. In the 1600s, *conversation* meant "citizenship." Today, it means "talking with others."[2]

Paul said, "For our *citizenship* is in heaven from where we look for our King to return to us one day."

We are citizens of heaven, not because we live or dwell there now. We are citizens because the King of heaven, Jesus Christ our Lord, dwells in us and is a citizen of our hearts. And, therefore, we are citizens of the heavenly land as *He* is a citizen there.

Until we make our home in our rightful land, however, we must live in a foreign environment. In this alien land, we need a place of security, a place of safety, a place of protection. That is God's *secret place* for us.

What *Is* a Secret Place?

A "secret" place is one remote from human travel. Estimates are that, by the year 2000, there will be seven billion people on earth. In 1988, Christians numbered 33 percent of the world's population. In any generation, no more than a third of the world has been Christian, according to missionary experts. An overall estimate is that, out

---

2 Vine, W.E., *Vine's Expository Dictionary of Old and New Testament Words* (Old Tappan: Fleming H. Revell Company, 1981), Vol. 1, p. 193.

of all the people who have lived since Christ died, was resurrected, and went to sit at the right hand of the Father, only about a fourth have counted themselves Christian.[3]

In terms of a personal relationship with Jesus, a genuinely born-again experience, the percentage is even lower. Not all who call themselves "Christian" are born again, unfortunately.

You can see that being *in* Him is a very secret place. Not many humans are frequenting the place called *in Him*. I am referring to all of those precious scriptures in the New Testament that tell us who we are in Christ Jesus, who we are *in Him*. (2 Cor. 5:17,21; Gal. 2:20; Rom. 8:1; Eph. 2:1-9.)

When Jesus really dwells in your heart by faith, and you begin to comprehend some things about love, you will start to understand what a verse such as Second Corinthians 5:21 really means.

That verse talks about a born-again person having been made the righteousness of God in Christ Jesus. Do you fully comprehend that? I doubt anyone really does. But if Jesus dwells in your heart by faith, you have a certain level of comprehension. If you dwell in that secret place of the Most High, you have an even better comprehension than thousands of born-again believers do.

In talking about that secret place, we might say it this way: "He that has Jesus dwelling in his heart, and who knows who he is *in Him*, shall abide under the shadow of the Almighty."

Is that true, or is that false? Is that consistent with the rest of the Word of God, or is it inconsistent? That statement is absolutely true and entirely consistent. If Jesus is dwelling in your heart by faith, and you know who you are in Him, then you abide under the shadow of the Almighty.

---

[3]Barrett, David B. *Cosmos, Chaos, and Gospel* (Birmingham: New Hope, Copyright 1987, Foreign Mission Board of the Southern Baptist Convention).

John 15:7 says:

If ye abide in me, and my words abide in you, ye shall ask what ye will, and it shall be done unto you.

That sounds to me like:

"If you abide in Me, and My words abide in you, you shall live in the protection of God."

That is the New Covenant way of saying, "He that dwelleth in the secret place of the Most High, shall abide under the shadow of the Almighty."

2

The Shadow of the Most High

Shall abide under the shadow of the Almighty.

Psalm 91:1

To abide under the shadow of God, you must dwell in the secret place of the Most High. And I do not want to pass over that phrase *the Most High* too quickly. Look at Philippians 2:5-11:

> **Let this mind be in you, which was also in Christ Jesus:**
>
> **Who, being in the form of God, thought it not robbery to be equal with God:**
>
> **But made himself of no reputation, and took upon him the form of a servant, and was made in the likeness of men:**
>
> **And being found in fashion as a man, he humbled himself, and became obedient unto death, even the death of the cross.**
>
> **Wherefore God also hath highly exalted him, and given him *a name which is above every name:***
>
> **That at the name of Jesus every knee should bow, of things in heaven, and things in earth, and things under the earth;**
>
> **And that every tongue should confess that Jesus Christ is Lord, to the glory of God the Father.**

A name which is above every name: Does that sound like *the Most High*? We are abiding in the One whose name has been exalted above every name that is named. We are

19

abiding in the One Who has the name to which every knee shall bow. He *is* "the Most High."

The person who meets these qualifications, the person who has Jesus dwelling in his heart, and knows who he is in Him, shall abide under the shadow of the Almighty. And what does that mean? That means you will live, you will abide, you will remain steadfast, you will go on being in the shadow of the Almighty. Believe me, the Almighty casts a powerful and wonderful shadow.

In the natural realm, a shadow is a definite area of shade cast upon a surface by something that intercepts the light rays. However, the Almighty's shadow is not a dark image. When we think of "a shadow," we think of something dark. We think of a shade.

Sunlight is brighter than any light that we give off, so the shadows we cast are dark. But suppose the light I gave off was brighter than sunlight? Then the shadow I cast would be light and not dark. When I walked outside, things would get brighter so that my shadow would be bright rather than dark.

That is the way Jesus' shadow has been since the Resurrection. He is brighter than the sun that hangs in our sky. Revelation 21:23 says that in the new earth, there will be no need of the sun nor the moon, for the Son of God will be the light.

His shadow is a bright shadow, not a dark one, for His light is greater than any natural light.

When you study the word *shadow* in the Greek language, you are directed to two passages: Matthew 17:1-7 and Acts 5:12-16.

> **And after six days, Jesus taketh Peter, James, and John his brother, and bringeth them up into an high mountain apart,**

And was transfigured before them: and his face did shine as the sun, and his raiment was white as the light.

And, behold, there appeared unto them Moses and Elias talking with him.

Then answered Peter, and said unto Jesus, Lord, it is good for us to be here: if thou wilt, let us make here three tabernacles; one for thee, and one for Moses, and one for Elias.

While he yet spake, behold, a bright cloud *overshadowed* them: and behold a voice out of the cloud, which said, 'This is my beloved Son, in whom I am well pleased; hear ye him.

And when the disciples heard it, they fell on their face, and were sore afraid.

Notice in the fifth verse, Matthew wrote that a *bright cloud overshadowed* them. The word *overshadowed* in the original is the Greek word for *shadow*. God's shadow does not cast a dark image. This is a *bright* cloud. God's shadow is light, not dark. Jesus and the three disciples were on a high mountain. The light of the Father, and now of the Son, is so bright that it outshines our sun.

Now look at the verses in Acts, the second reference to shadow that I mentioned above.

And by the hands of the apostles were many signs and wonders wrought among the people; (and they were all with one accord in Solomon's porch.

And of the rest durst no man join himself to them: but the people magnified them.

And believers were the more added to the Lord, multitudes both of men and women.)

Insomuch that they brought forth the sick into the streets, and laid them on beds and couches, that at the least the *shadow* of Peter passing by might overshadow some of them.

> There came also a multitude out of the cities round
> about unto Jerusalem, bringing sick folks, and them
> which were vexed with unclean spirits: and they were
> healed every one.

The Greek word used for *shadow* in verse 15 is the same word used in Matthew 17:5. The context here is not talking about the dark shadow Peter would have cast as he came in front of the rays of the sun. It is not talking about the normal, natural, dark shadow that his body would cast. But, by that time, Peter was dwelling in the secret place of the Most High so much that the very same kind of shadow that had been there at the Mount of Transfiguration was flowing through Peter. As that shadow passed over the people, every one of them was healed.

What Was the Transfiguration About?

In the past, as I studied the Transfiguration passages, I wondered, ''Why is that in the Bible? Jesus walked the earth as a man, anointed of the Holy Spirit. He did not operate in His Deity while here on earth. So what was the Transfiguration all about?''

I will guarantee you one thing: On the day when Peter walked down the street with his shadow falling on people, making them well, he had a much better understanding of the Transfiguration. The Transfiguration was a sign, an illustration, a very clear picture to us concerning Jesus. It shows us we can dwell *in Him* so the overshadowing of God will be such a part of our lives that it is clear we are involved in eternity right now.

You do not have to die to be involved in eternity. If you did, the Transfiguration never could have taken place. Instead, that would be the one time when Jesus took back His Deity and did something completely out of character for His human nature. And we know that did not happen.

Each Christian's goal in life should be to have Jesus so dwelling in his or her heart by faith that more and more comprehension of that secret place *in Him* would be possible.

Psalm 91:1 actually is saying:

"He that lives under the shadow of the greater One, with the Word in his heart, shall abide under the active, creative, energizing, healing, powerful flow of the anointing of Almighty God."

Now that is a "mouthful," I know, but it is true. That is really what is being said to us as new creatures in Christ Jesus, New Covenant people who walk in the light of what God has given us.

Expect Miracles!

Peter did not have "a corner" on this. Yes, we can expect things like that in our lives. I dare you to expect!

The shadow of the Almighty is a bright cloud, a wonderful shadow. All kinds of things happen when you are under the shadow of the Almighty. What this means is that everywhere Peter walked, that shadow followed him, because he was abiding under it. Everywhere Peter went, the shadow of the Almighty went.

Let's get Christ dwelling in our hearts by faith, daily. Let's learn and comprehend more and more of who we are *in Him*. Peter did not sit down one day and figure out how to get God's shadow to overshadow him. He just got involved with the fact that Jesus was dwelling in his heart.

And remember: This is the same Peter who denied His Lord three times on the day of Jesus' crucifixion. This is old unfaithful Peter, who cursed in a courtyard while Jesus was inside the house being tried. Yet Peter is the one who walked down the road with his shadow overshadowing people so that they rose up healed.

So do not rule yourself out of this kind of miracle. Do not say, "Oh, I'm so unworthy. I could never do that." Let Jesus dwell in your heart, and learn more and more of who you are *in Him*. Then let the rest of it take care of itself.

Thank God we do lay hands on the sick, and they recover. Thank God that as we agree in prayer, people are healed and financial needs are met. But there is a whole lot more that God wants to do in and through us, if we will just put ourselves in a place where He can. Learn how to find that secret place.

3

My Refuge and My Fortress

. . . He is my refuge and my fortress.

Psalm 91:2

As I read Psalm 91:2, more Old Testament than New Testament verses come to mind. There is nothing wrong with Old Testament verses, but at first, I wondered why there were not more verses in the New Testament that confirmed this second verse of Psalm 91.

A word study, however, revealed why there were more verses in the Old Testament having to do with *refuge* and *fortress*. The Old Testament was written in Hebrew, and in those times, there was more occasion to desire and look for places of shelter from trouble.

In the New Testament, there is little mention of such places. In fact, there is only one use of *refuge*, and that is in Hebrews 6:18. The word *fortress* is not found at all in the New Testament.

So, under the New Covenant, we have to look for some words or phrases that convey the idea of a spiritual hiding place instead of a literal hiding place.

What *is* a refuge? According to a dictionary, *refuge* is "shelter or protection from danger, difficulty; a place of safety; shelter; safe retreat; action taken to escape trouble or difficulty."[1]

---

[1]*New World Dictionary*, Second College Edition.

25

Here are some New Testament verses that describe this kind of spiritual place:

For in Him we live, and move, and have our being.

Acts 17:28a

There hath no temptation taken you but such as is common to man: but God is faithful, who will not suffer you to be tempted above that ye are able; but will with the temptation also make *a way to escape* (a refuge), that ye may be able to bear it.

1 Corinthians 10:13

There are things that you are going to face in your life that are common to man. For example — death. No one likes to talk about death, but it is one thing that certainly is common to man. Your family members and friends are going to die. You are going to die. I am going to die. Unless the Lord returns in our time, all of us will go through the experience of physical death.

I believe that, unless Jesus returns, I am going to live a long time because the last verse of Psalm 91 says **with long life will I satisfy him.** I do not know how long my life will have to be for me to be satisfied, but I know it has not been long enough yet! However, if Jesus tarries, some day I will die a physical death.

Here are some other things that are common to man:

- Not everyone will be saved.
- People will try to take advantage of you and misuse you.
- You will be criticized.
- Satan will try to make you sick.
- Satan will attack your finances.

You will never find yourself in a position where you can say truthfully, ''No one has ever gone through this before.''

But, no matter what you face, *God is faithful*. (1 Cor. 1:9.) We have a *refuge*, a way of escape, and we can bear the things that happen. I am not saying we can *stand* the things that happen — stay sick, broke, hurt, or defeated. I do not mean that. No! I mean that under the New Covenant, when we come to Jesus, our refuge, we find ourselves in the secret place of the Most High.

Who Misses It — You or God?

A lady came to me once and asked me about a very bad circumstance which had happened in her life.

She said, "I did everything I knew to do. I believed everything I knew to believe. I said everything I knew to say. I was as strong in faith as I knew how to be. Why did it happen? Why?"

I shared a lot of things with her that I am sharing with you in this book. First of all, the "way of escape" is not turning around and running. The "way of escape" does not lie in turning from the Word to bitterness. The "way of escape" is not to say, "Well, the Word didn't work," and walk away from the Bible.

When you go to the Word of God and begin looking for a way to escape, the way will lead you right back to the Word, solidly, completely. Jesus told us the way of escape: *If ye abide in me, and my words abide in you* (John 15:7).

You will find that, no matter what Satan throws your way, no matter what he brings across your pathway, when you look for a way to escape, it is in the Word.

The lady I mentioned was dealing with a lot of bitterness. As the devil kept on attacking again and again, there were many times when she should have gone to the Word. Instead, she only held on to what she already knew.

I do not think I am a hard person, but I have to tell the truth according to the Word. I did not say what I did to her to be hard, but either God's Word is true, or it is not true. Either that lady somehow missed finding her way to escape, or God missed it — and God has never missed it. His Word is true. There *is* a refuge.

You may say, "Do you mean to tell me that you are so hard and cruel you would tell that woman she missed it?"

I made sure she knew that I did not mean to be hard and did not want to be cruel. But there are only two alternatives: She missed it, or God missed it. I would rather point out to her that she must have missed it than tell God He did!

You say, "Well, what *is* the answer then? If someone is doing their best to live their life according to everything they know and understand about God's Word in a life or death situation and misses it, can any of us ever live according to the Bible?"

Yes, we absolutely can. That is the reason I keep teaching the Word and teaching the Word, because it takes a continuous intake of the Word to make our spirits strong. Then, when the devil brings something against us, we can know how to find the way to escape. Reading the Word once a week is not enough. In fact, two or three times a week is not enough. Being involved in the Word must be a way of life. You must *live* in the Word.

Sometimes, people are inclined to think that "following Jesus" means selling the car, the furniture, the house, and going into the ministry. But there is a much deeper meaning than that. The real way to follow Him is to take hold of His Word and make it mean everything to you, so much so that if you are confronted with a lady like I was faced with, there is nothing but the Word to say to her.

I sat in my chair across the desk from her and squirmed. I tried to offer her some other answer. I will be honest. My mind brought up some things I had learned in seminary about comforting people. I thought this would be a good time to bring out some of those things.

But I suddenly discovered how much the Word had become a part of me, because there was not anything else to say but that God's Word is true, and He did not miss it. I would hope I never have to say anything like that again to someone in turmoil, someone who is hurting. However, if the same situation arises, I will have to say the same thing.

The best help I could give her, the kindest thing I could do for her, was show her that she *had* missed it. I could show her that even when we do miss the way to escape, you have to face it and get back in the Word in order to recover. There is a way to escape when you have missed the way to escape! That is to always come back to the Word of God and believe your way out of your situation.

If you do not find the way to escape, it is not God's fault. It is never God's fault.

Any time you depart from the Word, if you want what God has in the Word to minister to you, you will have to come back to it. Any time you walk away from God's Word, any time you miss it, there is only one way to get His benefits working again in your life, and that is to come right back where you missed it, line up with God's Word, and go on from there. If you are not willing to do that, then you cannot ever expect the great things God has said in this book to work in your life.

New Covenant Believers Are Different

In the times covered by the Old Testament, believers were always running. Moses ran. Elijah ran. Jonah ran. David ran. Danger threatened, and they hunted a refuge in the earth, a place to hide. And God hid them in caves or in the wilderness — except in Jonah's case.

The others were running from earthly danger, but Jonah was running from God's call on his life. The Almighty will not provide a refuge *for* disobedience. However, He will provide a place of repentance. God did provide Jonah a refuge from destruction, as well — the belly of a whale.

The picture of the New Testament believer is very different. We are not told to run to a natural refuge. We are told to *stand*.

> **Wherefore take unto you the whole armour of God, that ye may be able to withstand in the evil day, and having done all, to stand.**
>
> **Stand therefore . . . .**
>
> Ephesians 6:13,14

Abide in Him; get His Word abiding in you, and *stand*. Resist the devil, and he will run from you. (James 4:7.) Instead of always running from the enemy as they had to in the Old Testament, thank God, we are to take our places in Him and *stand* against the enemy.

I used to wonder how long we have to stand, but I finally figured that out. Do you want to know how long to stand? You must *stand* until the way to escape is right in front of you. That is how long.

The reason it takes so long for most of us to find the way to escape is that it takes us so long to decide to stand. It takes so long to put on the armor of God. Most people want to count all of the time they were putting on the armor as *standing*. However, the standing time does not start until you *take on* the whole armor of God. (Eph. 6:11.)

Many Christians only have on the helmet of salvation, and they think they are standing. You do not have on the whole armor until you abide in Jesus and His words abide in you. Remember: A sword goes with that armor, and the sword is the Word of God. (Eph. 6:17.)

You do not begin to stand until you are fully dressed in your armor and have the Word of God on the inside of you ready to use. And about the time you get ready for battle and begin to stand, you will find the way to escape is there!

I have found that it always works that way. The reason I know so well is that I have been there. I have tried to stand without the whole armor, and it does not work. On the other hand, I have put on the whole armor and seen the devil flee when I took my stand. The Word of God makes it clear that the devil *will* flee from us under those circumstances. He will run as in terror.

Hundreds of times I have had people tell me, "I resisted the devil, and he didn't flee. Why didn't he flee?"

There are a number of possible reasons, but none of those reasons are that the Word does not work. The Word always is true. More than likely, those people who thought they were resisting the devil were not using the Word of God. Also, that demon may have been yelling, as he was running away, "I'm not leaving." The devil and all of his troops are liars. They will leave when you resist them, because the Word says so.

Psalm 91 is not for everyone, and those who make it a way of life may find themselves being called "fanatics." Other people will call them "stuck up," or "high and mighty." But what it amounts to is that you either make God's Word a way of life, or you do not. When you make it a way of life, the Word works.

If the Word is not working in your life, then you have not made the Bible a way of life.

People who say, "It's not working for me," should realize that they really are saying, "The Word is not a way of life to me."

Once I got a five-page, single-spaced letter from a lady who said, "I just want you to know I'm not confessing the Word anymore. I'm not talking the Word anymore. I'm not standing on the Word anymore. I'm just telling it like it is."

That was really too bad. You see, she had made a choice. The Word was not going to be a way of life to her. If she thought she had problems before, I really hate to think what her life was like once she began to get in agreement with her problems instead of with the Lord.

Our Fortress Is Doing the Word

You have seen that the word *refuge* is only in the New Testament once. The word *fortress* is not in there at all. However, a *fortress* is simply a strong place of protection from which you can fight the enemy.

That definition does remind me of some New Testament verses:

> Not everyone that saith unto me, Lord, Lord shall enter into the kingdom of heaven; but he that doeth the will of My Father which is in heaven.
>
> Many will say to me in that day, Lord, Lord, have we not prophesied in thy name? and in thy name have cast out devils? and in thy name done many wonderful works?
>
> And then will I profess unto them, I never knew you: depart from me, ye that work iniquity.
>
> Therefore whosoever heareth these sayings of mine, and doeth them, I will liken him unto a wise man, which built his house upon a rock:
>
> And the rain descended, and the floods came, and the winds blew, and beat upon that house; and it fell not: for it was founded upon a rock.
>
> Matthew 7:21-25

The fortress talked about in the 91st Psalm, to a New Covenant believer, is *hearing* and *doing* the words of Jesus. Simply knowing the words, singing the words, or saying the words will not place you in a strong fortress. The strength comes in *doing* the Word that you know.

The reason you are like a house built on rock when you hear and do the sayings of Jesus is that *He* is the Rock. When you know His teachings and do His words, you are built upon Him, and He becomes your fortress, your rock.

Psalm 18:1,2 presents this truth even in Old Testament times:

I will love thee, O Lord, my strength.

The Lord is my rock, and my fortress, and my deliverer; my God, my strength, in whom I will trust; my buckler, and the horn of my salvation, and my high tower.

In Deuteronomy, Moses wrote the same thing in these words:

How should one chase a thousand, and two put ten thousand to flight, except their Rock had sold them, and the Lord had shut them up?

For their rock is not as our Rock, even our enemies themselves being judges.

Deuteronomy 32:30,31

Their *rock* was a sand pile, a house built out of sand. Their rock is Satan, and he always runs when you stand up to him, so that all of those serving him have their foundations pulled out from under them.

I realize this verse was referring to Israel's literal, physical enemies. But beyond the people fighting Israel, Moses was talking about their "rock," who was a heathen god, a demon. He said their "rock" had sold them out.

There were two kinds of "rocks" then, and there are two kinds of "rocks" now. Their rock sold them, and our Rock bought us. He will never desert us.

There are people you will meet tomorrow, people you will talk to on the phone, people who will come into your place of business who have a rock all right! But if they could only see their rock, they would discover it is nothing but a sand pile. Their rock is Satan. They may be fighting you with everything they have.

However, when you, a born-again believer, take a firm stand against the enemy, who is their rock, their god, their strength, their refuge, he will leave them. Many times believers encounter unbelievers and try to deal with their unfair ways, with their trying to take advantage. But, if believers could just realize that taking a firm stand against the enemy would cause him to desert those people, then the opposition would cease.

No matter how much they want to put you down, say no to what you need, or take advantage of you, they are standing on sand. Your Rock, on the other hand, will never, never desert you.

Now, who are you going to trust? Who are you going to make your refuge and fortress?

4

He Will Deliver You

**Surely he shall deliver thee from the snare
of the fowler, and from the noisome pestilence.**

Psalm 91:3

Before we begin to discuss this verse, there are four words that I want to define: *snare, fowler, noisome,* and *pestilence.*

A *snare* is a trap for small animals, but it also can be anything dangerous or risky in your spiritual walk.

A *snare* is anything that tempts or attracts you, but it will catch you by the foot — so to speak — and prevent you from walking on with the Lord.

A *snare* is a trap set by the enemy and can be anything that entangles a Christian in sinful behavior or attitudes.

A *fowler* is the word used in England for a person who hunts, traps, or shoots wild birds. Today, in the United States, we usually call this person "a sportsman" or a hunter.

The third word that readers sometimes have difficulty with is *noisome.* We generally think of that as someone who is noisy. However, in this case, it means something that smells bad and is offensive. Also, something that is *noisome* can be something dangerous.

Many Christians think the way I did at one time about this phrase *noisome pestilence.* Once I saw part of a movie about swarms of locusts covering a certain place. Since they were pests and very noisy, I thought that sort of thing was what the third verse of Psalm 91 meant.

35

However, a *pestilence*, I have found, really is a plague, a fatal or contagious disease.

The first thing to notice about this verse is something typical of the Old Testament. The psalmist wrote, **Surely he shall deliver thee**. Of course *He* refers to God Almighty, the Most High. But the tense in the psalm is future: He *will* deliver you.

Since the Day of Pentecost, those promises have become past tense for those of us under the New Covenant: He already *has* delivered us.

The psalmist believed that God *would* deliver him. He had to put it in future tense because it had not yet happened. His statements became affirmations to future generations.

"Don't get into worrying, because the Most High *will* deliver you from all of the traps and plagues of the enemy."

Today, deliverance already has been accomplished. Too many Christians are still praying future prayers. They are not walking in the faith available to them through the knowledge that Jesus already has won the war and the victory.

The way to pray in faith is not, "Lord, I know that you *will*," but "Lord, I know that you *have* already delivered me."

New Covenant believers must read the 91st Psalm in the past tense, not as future tense, the way it was written by the author. You *have been* delivered from the snare of the "fowler," the devil. You are not looking for something to happen. You are bringing your thoughts, attitudes, and actions in line with something that already has happened.

Many people are still asking, expecting, even begging God to do what He says already has been done. When they do that, it is a clear sign of one of two things: They are ignorant, and the Lord said ignorance would destroy His people (Hos. 4:6), or they are into doubt and disbelief. In that case, the Holy Spirit wrote through the Apostle James, they will receive nothing from the Lord. (James 1:6,7.)

Years ago, when I ministered, I would have people who needed healing come to the front to have hands laid on them. Then I would pray for God to heal them.

One day, the Lord stopped me and said, "Don't pray that way any longer. I have said in My Word that I have already healed them. (1 Pet. 2:24.) Tell their bodies to come in line with My Word. I am not the problem; My Word is not the problem; their bodies are the problems. If their bodies will get in line with the Word, healing will manifest in them."

From then on, that has been the way I have prayed for people.

The Devil Is the Fowler

As I mentioned before, obviously, the devil is the fowler in the lives of New Covenant believers. He is the one who "hunts, traps, and shoots" Christians. So, in this word picture painted by the psalmist, we must be the birds! The devil is the one who tries to tempt or attract us into things that are dangerous and risky to our spiritual growth, things that are traps for us.

Look at James 1:12-16:

> **Blessed is the man that endureth temptation: for when he is tried, he shall receive the crown of life, which the Lord hath promised to them that love him.**
>
> **Let no man say when he is tempted, I am tempted of God: for God cannot be tempted with evil, neither tempteth he any man:**
>
> **But every man is tempted, when he is drawn away of his own lust, and enticed.**
>
> **Then when lust hath conceived, it bringeth forth sin: and sin, when it is finished, bringeth forth death.**
>
> **Do not err, my beloved brethren.**

First of all, these verses say that the person who *endures* temptation is blessed. James did not say that the person who yields, then repents and recovers to rise above his sin is blessed. When you do not fall for the temptation — the *snare* set before you — you are blessed.

James 1:13 specifically spells out that God is not the tempter. He does not set the snare. The devil sets the trap, but only man can trip it. I am not a hunter or a trapper, but I understand a little bit about rabbit traps.

Suppose a man makes a rabbit trap and sets it some place where there is supposed to be rabbits. All he does is set the trap. He does not catch the rabbit. In fact, the trap does not reach out and catch the rabbit. *The rabbit catches himself.*

Any animal caught in a snare is there because he has given in to temptation and reached for the bait, thus getting himself caught in whatever kind of trap has been set. So all the devil does is set the trap and place the temptation out there as bait. When a Christian is drawn into the trap by his own lust (James 1:14), then he is caught.

That is why *you* are responsible. No matter what kind of trap the devil has set, you are accountable for falling into it.

I believe that thousands of years ago, the devil designed every form of sin and set it in motion. As far as most sin goes, he does not have to do anything anymore. He set the various kinds of traps ages ago, and men come along and fall into them.

Other men see how attractive these traps are. They see how to gain a personal profit from making them. So they work to make the devil's snares look more enticing and more desirable. They prey on their fellow men and gain profit from the entrapment of others by making the ''bait'' taste better.

All the devil is doing now, in most cases, is watching his traps. Man keeps getting himself caught in them again and again.

The Apostle was inspired to stick that one little sentence in there: **Do not err, my beloved brethren** (James 1:16). If it were not possible for you to keep from getting into error (the snare), that verse would not be in the Word.

An Old Testament verse about being snared is Proverbs 6:2: **Thou art snared with the words of thy mouth.**

If the snare is sin, how does this proverb about words fit?

The answer may sound hard, but it is truth. Anything you speak that is contradictory to the Word of God is a lie. Anything you speak that is not in line with the Word, anything you say that is contradictory to God can be a snare to you. You are entrapped by the words you speak, or you are victorious by the words you speak. (James 3:5-8; Prov. 18:21.)

Look at Galatians 5:1:

> **Stand fast therefore in the liberty wherewith Christ hath made us free, and be not entangled again with the yoke of bondage.**

Also, look at Ephesians 6:16:

> **Above all, taking the shield of faith, wherewith ye shall be able to quench all the fiery darts of the wicked one.**

The *wicked one* is the devil. Here he is described as "shooting" at us. So definitely, the devil is the fowler, the hunter of men's souls. But remember this: God *has* delivered us from the snare of the fowler.

You Can Rise Above Sin

Many Christians want to take the attitude of "I can't help it." But, if you do sin, it is not because you could not help it. God has already "helped" it. He already has defeated the devil and raised you above sin. If sin has become a part of your life, it is by your own choice to "take the bait" in the trap. You made a decision to agree with the fowler or with God, and that decision determined whether you were caught or escaped.

I wrestled with this truth for a long time because of my religious background as a child. I did not want to sin. It was not my desire nor my plan. I just thought that somewhere down the line, the devil was going to throw a temptation in front of me that somehow I could not overcome.

But the Word clearly shows that there is not one single temptation the devil can place in front of you that you cannot overcome. (1 Cor. 10:13.)

I suppose I must have thought subconsciously that there were some temptations left out of the atonement! I must have assumed there were some kinds of temptation that escaped when Jesus died on the cross. But there are none.

Many Christians today apparently still have this same assumption operating in their minds. I can tell you of a certainty, however, that if you keep moving toward the Son of God, keep making the Word a way of life, a year from now many of those things that tempt you today will not be a temptation any longer. You *have been* delivered from the devil's snares.

Galatians 5:1 tells us that we can rise above sin:

Stand fast therefore in the liberty wherewith Christ hath made us free.

Obviously, you can rise above temptation and sin, or the Apostle Paul would not have told us to stand fast in the liberty with which Jesus has made us free.

Another fact about the devil that always excites me is found in Luke 10:17,18:

And the seventy returned again with joy, saying, Lord, even the devils are subject unto us through thy name.

And he said unto them, I beheld Satan as lightning fall from heaven.

Jesus, the Son of God, while on earth in His mortal body, told the disciples that He *had* seen the devil fall from heaven. That incident had to have happened at least 4,000 years before Jesus made that statement.

That was kind of a "put down," if you think about it. There were 70 disciples jumping up and down with joy, excited because the demons were subject to them through Jesus' name.

And Jesus just kind of shrugged His shoulders and said, "So what? I saw him fall thousands of years ago. It's no big deal."

Today, it has been at least 6,000 years since Satan fell from heaven. God did not have to wait for Jesus to die on the cross to defeat the devil. He had been defeated in the heavenlies. But Adam and Eve's sin allowed the devil to win a place in the lives of mankind and over the systems of the world. The sacrifice of the Lamb of God on the cross defeated Satan in the lives of men. He has been twice defeated, and the third and final time is coming up.

Jesus translated the promises of Psalm 91 into past tense when He said:

Behold, I give you power to tread on serpents and scorpions, and over *all* the power of the enemy: and nothing shall by any means hurt you.

Luke 10:19

We need to get a clear understanding of the fact that whether the devil is hunting, trapping, or shooting, nothing shall by any means hurt us. Yet so many Christians live as if they are not sure the devil has been defeated. They look at how strong he comes on, how hard he attacks, and how hard the things he brings against them are to overcome. However, if they once see how defeated he is, those things will not seem so strong or hard.

The Apostle Matthew reported the same fact about Jesus a little differently in his gospel:

> **And Jesus came and spake unto them, saying, All power is given unto me in heaven and in earth.**
>
> **Go ye therefore, and teach all nations, baptizing them in the name of the Father, and of the Son, and of the Holy Ghost:**
>
> **Teaching them to observe all things whatsoever I have commanded you: and, lo, I am with you alway, even unto the end of the world. Amen.**
>
> **Matthew 28:18-20**

Matthew reported that Jesus said *all* power had been given to Him in heaven and in the earth. Then in Luke 10:19, it is recorded that Jesus said, ''I give my followers power over all of the power of the enemy.'' He could do that because God had given all power to Him.

The complete ''declaration of freedom'' from Satan is found in Mark 16:15-18:

> **And he said unto them, Go ye into all the world, and preach the gospel to every creature.**
>
> **He that believeth and is baptized shall be saved; but he that believeth not shall be damned.**
>
> **And these signs shall follow them that believe; In my name shall they cast out devils; they shall speak with new tongues;**
>
> **They shall take up serpents; and if they drink any deadly thing, it shall not hurt them; they shall lay hands on the sick, and they shall recover.**

Jesus is saying that we have total deliverance from Satan. So when we declare that He *has* delivered us from the snare of the fowler, we are including all of the things mentioned in the above verses of scripture. We have total and complete deliverance.

You may say, "Well, I know Jesus has delivered us, but the devil comes again and again. He just keeps saying these things to my mind. I know what the Word of God says, but how can I deal with the fact that the devil keeps coming against me?"

Satan is a *Noisome Pestilence*

Satan is noisy, foul-smelling, offensive, and a pest. He is the source of fatal contagious diseases in the natural and contagious errors of doctrines in the spiritual. But we have been delivered.

The devil wants to defeat us. He did not defeat Jesus, but he thinks he can defeat those who are members of Jesus' Body — and he can, *if we let him.*

He wants to put sickness — contagious and fatal diseases on us. But Matthew 8:17 and 1 Peter 2:24 clearly say that Jesus took those things for us. Therefore, we no longer have to have them.

Think about cancer, which is usually called a "terminal disease." I believe the thing that brings the greatest fear to most men and women is hearing those words, "You have a terminal disease. You have a fatal disease. There is no cure known to man."

That is not a true statement and never will be. The cure *is* known to man, and that is Jesus. We *have been* delivered from the noisome pestilence. Cancer is a pestilence, and the world is full of fear of it. But the Word declares that we have been freed from it.

There is not one fatal disease, not one contagious disease, that we have not been delivered from.

The devil also wants to get us into doubt, disbelief, and errors of doctrine. But he has been defeated there also, for the Word says:

> **All scripture is given by inspiration of God, and is profitable for doctrine, for reproof, for correction, for instruction in righteousness: That the man of God may be perfect, and thoroughly furnished unto all good works.**
>
> **2 Timothy 3:16**

So the devil comes back to your mind again and again and again? Just remember that he probably is the noisiest being in existence. He may come and speak the same things to your mind over and over. However, *if you will believe what the Bible says and tell him to leave, you can effectively resist him,* and he will flee. That means he will run away so far that you cannot hear him.

Romans 12:2 says:

> **And be not conformed to this world: but be ye transformed by the renewing of your mind, that ye may prove what is that good, and acceptable, and perfect, will of God.**

That means many things, but one of them is this: If you have your mind renewed (Rom. 12:2), you have resisted the devil. He has fled, and your mind is no longer full of his doubts.

The person who knows who he is in Christ Jesus abides under the shadow of the Almighty in a place that is full of God's anointing, God's power, God's working. Thus the Word of God becomes your refuge and your fortress, because your trust is in God and His Word.

When you can truly say that and mean it, you are saying that you have been delivered from the snare of the fowler. You have been delivered from anything Satan would try to do in your life. We are living in the blessing of what Jesus has already done.

The responsibility that falls on us is simply to bring our lives in line with what Jesus already has done. We do that by faith in God's Word, by believing what it says, saying what it says, and walking in the fullness of it.

5

Feathers May Not Be Enough

**He shall cover thee with His feathers,
and under His wings shalt thou trust:
his truth shall be thy shield and buckler.**

Psalm 91:4

When I read that fourth verse, I always think of an incident I heard about once. The story goes that a woman was standing on the street corner one night in downtown Fort Worth, Texas. All of the stores had closed, so it was after dark. She was alone and waiting for a bus.

She said her handbag was one of those oversized ones, and she had it slung over her shoulder. As she stood there alone, a man walked up and kind of eased over next to her. Then he grabbed that big purse, trying to take it away from her.

As she grappled with him, hanging onto her purse, she tried to think of some scripture to claim or something to say. All she could think of was Psalm 91:4 — and only one word of that verse came to her!

So she began to yell at the top of her voice, "Feathers, feathers, feathers, feathers!"

In a few seconds, the man gave her a real odd look, as you can well imagine. Then he turned loose of her purse and ran off as hard as he could go. This actually happened. I have met this lady.

If the Word really works that way, it is worth looking into! However, *you* may not be able to deal with danger by just screaming, "Feathers."

How Does God "Cover" You?

The Word says, **He shall cover thee.** Usually when we think of the word *cover*, we have in mind putting something on, or putting something over or in front of something else. The idea usually is to conceal, hide, or protect something. And there are several Hebrew words that carry that particular meaning.

However, the Hebrew word translated *cover* in verse 4 is a different word. It is *sakak*, and it is only used four times as *cover* in the entire Old Testament. There are perhaps a dozen other places where it appears in variations such as *covered, covereth, or covered*, but always with the primary meaning of "to entwine as a screen." By implication, it means "to defend, hedge in, join together, set, shut up" in an enclosure.[1]

Let's look at one place where two different Hebrew words are translated *cover*, in order to see the different meanings.

In Exodus 40:17-19, Moses wrote:

> **And it came to pass in the first month in the second year, on the first day of the month, that the tabernacle was reared up.**
>
> **And Moses reared up the tabernacle, and fastened his sockets, and set up the boards thereof, and put in the bars thereof, and reared up his pillars.**
>
> **And he spread abroad the tent over the tabernacle, and put the *covering* of the tent above upon it; as the Lord commanded Moses.**

Here the word *covering* has the meaning that we generally attribute to it: Moses put the covering over the

---

[1]Strong, James. *The New Strong's Exhaustive Concordance of the Bible* (Nashville: Thomas Nelson Publishers, 1984), "Hebrew and Chaldee Dictionary," p. 82, #5526.

tent. The Hebrew word is *mikceh*, meaning covering, such as "weather-boarding."[2]

But in Exodus 40:21, the word sakak is used:

> **And he brought the ark into the tabernacle, and set up the vail of the *covering*, and *covered* the ark of the testimony; as the Lord commanded Moses.**

As we saw from the Hebrew, *Sakak* does not mean simply "to hide or to conceal," but "to hedge in." Moses did not lay the veil over the ark as a covering. The veil was a very thick curtain that divided a small inner room from the two outer courts. The Ark of the Covenant was "hedged in" behind that veil.

Most of us think of God covering us so that the devil will never see us again. We will be completely hidden, and the devil cannot find us to do anything to us. But this verse is not talking about that kind of covering. God has not promised to hide you so the devil cannot find you.

What God is promising is to *hedge you in*. He will "cover you with His feathers," a word picture of a hen covering her little chicks protectively. As long as you stay inside that hedge, the enemy cannot harm you. However, if you stray *outside* the hedge, you not only are not hidden, you are not protected!

The enemy knows you are there in that hedge. He can hear you, and perhaps he can see you. But he cannot get to you as long as you remain behind the hedge.

The Ark of the Covenant was completely cut off — not to hide it, but to keep people away from it. Only the high priest was allowed in the holy of holies.

---

[2]Strong. *Hebrew and Chaldee Dictionary*, p. 66, #4372.

Satan Is Not Omnipresent

Satan is limited to being in one place at one time. He is not omnipresent, as God is. One place in the Bible that clearly shows this fact is the book of Job.

> Now there was a day when the sons of God came to present themselves before the Lord, and Satan came also among them.
>
> And the Lord said unto Satan, Whence comest thou? Then Satan answered the Lord, and said, From going to and fro in the earth, and from walking up and down in it.
>
> Job 1:6,7

You can see that when you are going to and fro, walking up and down, you are moving from one place to another, not being in all places at once. And that is what the enemy is doing today, constantly moving all over the face of the earth.

> And the Lord said unto Satan, Hast thou considered my servant Job, that there is none like him in the earth, a perfect and an upright man, one that feareth God, and escheweth evil?
>
> Then Satan answered the Lord, and said, Doth Job fear God for nought?
>
> Hast not thou made an *hedge* about him, and about his house, and about all that he hath on every side? thou hast blessed the work of his hands, and his substance is increased in the land.
>
> But put forth thine hand now, and touch all that he hath, and he will curse thee to thy face.
>
> And the Lord said unto Satan, Behold, all that he hath is in thy power; only upon himself put not forth thine hand. So Satan went forth from the presence of the Lord.
>
> Job 1:8-12

Notice that, in verse 10, Satan is quoted as using the word *hedge*. This is yet a different Hebrew word, *suwk*, literally meaning "shut in (for formation, protection, or restraint):— fence, (make an) hedge (up)."[3]

God did not deny that he had put a hedge around Job, a hedge that apparently looked to Satan like an impregnable fence. When we think about a hedge, we think about shrubbery. We think of bushes that are only a few feet high, bushes that it is possible to make a way through. Little boys, dogs, and cats are always making paths through most of the kinds of hedges we know.

But the hedge God had placed around Job looked like a great, high fence to Satan. He knew there was no way he could get beyond it, although he could see Job within it. He could see Job prospering inside God's fence. Satan was complaining to God about this fence that surrounded Job, his family, and everything that belonged to him.

He is saying, "I can't do anything to Job. You have a fence around him. No wonder he 'fears' (loves, respects, is in awe of) you. How do you know he would do this if he were out in the open where I could tempt and test him?"

Job lived in Old Testament times. In fact, most scholars believe that Job is the oldest book in the Bible, which means it had to be written long before Moses took the children of Israel out of Egypt.

Long before Satan tried to tempt Jesus after His forty-day fast in the wilderness, he tried to subtly tempt God. Here he challenged God to test Job:

> **But put forth thine hand now, and touch all that he hath, and he will curse thee to thy face.**
>
> **Job 1:11**

---

[3]Strong. "Hebrew and Chaldee Dictionary," p. 113, #7753.

Satan was suggesting that God be the reason for Job's destruction. He wanted to tempt God into making a move against Job in order to prove His point: that Job loved Him wholeheartedly for himself. And God would not do it. The devil is so full of pride that he still thinks he is smarter than God!

This ought to be evidence to anyone that God does not bring sickness and disease or poverty on His children. This one verse ought to show that God does not wipe out His people. Satan challenged Him to on this one occasion, at least, and God refused.

However, God allowed Satan to touch everything Job had — not because God wondered what Job would do, but as a lesson for Satan. Also, Job's faith was much stronger after all of this was over.

Notice that God still kept the hedge around Job personally. Satan could not kill Job. A lot of Christians are afraid Satan is going to kill them. But, although Satan could attack everything Job had, he could not touch his life. There are many different views on the book of Job, which I cannot get into in this book. I want to concentrate on one thing: God's hedge around Job.

God Has a Hedge Around Us

God has a similar hedge around us, and I will show you that under the New Covenant. When God established your redemption in the Lord Jesus Christ, He built a huge hedge around you and cut you off from spiritual death, poverty, and sickness and disease.

Satan can see you inside that fence, and he can hear you. However, he cannot get to you unless you come outside it through your choices. As long as you walk in the light of your redemption, Satan cannot cross that hedge. We have a greater hedge than Job did! *Nothing shall by any means hurt us.* (Luke 10:19.)

The second phrase of Psalm 91:4 says, **and under his wings shalt thou** *trust.* So trusting God has a big part in your protection. I do not know anyone who has seen this hedge of the Lord's. I do not know exactly what it looks like. All of this is a matter of *trust.* I believe in the redemption of the Lord Jesus Christ. I trust God's Word, and so I walk boldly by faith. It is all a matter of trusting what God said in His Word.

And the last part of that verse is: **his truth shall be thy shield and buckler.** What is His truth? His truth is His Word. Remember, Ephesians 6:16 says to take the shield of faith to quench all the fiery darts of the wicked. What develops your shield of faith? Faith comes by hearing the Word of God. (Rom. 10:17.) As you hear His truths in the Word, your shield of faith is formed and developed.

Why do you need a shield of faith? If you are inside the hedge, if the adversary cannot get over or through the fence, you may think you do not need a shield. Well, there is one more word in Psalm 91:4 that we have not talked about, and that is *buckler.*

There are four different Hebrew words translated in the *King James Version* as *buckler.* The first three mean a shield, or a larger shield, or a javelin — so that could mean some kind of shield with a weapon. However, none of those three is the word used here.

The word is *cocherah,* and it is only used this one time in the Old Testament. It means "something surrounding the person."[4] So this *buckler* the psalmist is referring to is a hedge that completely surrounds a person.

Your shield of faith, however, is the devil's target! If you are within that surrounding hedge, or shield of faith, then he cannot directly attack you. All he can do is shoot

---

[4]Strong. "Hebrew and Chaldee Dictionary," p. 82, #5507.

fiery darts at your shield. He just keeps shooting at that target.

So if God's truth is your buckler, and the shield of faith is developed by hearing the truth, what is Satan shooting at all of the time? He is shooting at the Word of God. So keep your shield of faith intact. Stay in the Word, and those darts of the enemy will just fall off harmlessly.

I picture that shield of faith as a huge waterfall right there in front of me all the time, because Ephesians 5:26 talks about the cleansing of the Church **with the washing of water by the word.** I stay behind God's wonderful waterfall which surrounds me, right inside God's hedge.

Do you see how your offensive weapon works when you use it? Here you are inside the hedge, behind the shield of faith, and all of Satan's fiery darts are flying right into your shield of faith and being quenched immediately. Every now and then, you just reach out with the sword of the Spirit and give the enemy one good chop. Lay the Word out before you.

For one last scripture concerning this truth, let's look at 1 Timothy 6:12:

> **Fight the good fight of faith, lay hold on eternal life, whereunto thou art also called, and hast professed a good profession before many witnesses.**

I believe we always ought to make a good *profession*, so if you agree, pray this prayer with your whole heart:

> *Thank You, Lord, that I am redeemed from spiritual death. I am redeemed from the curse of the law. I am redeemed from sickness and disease. I am redeemed from poverty and destruction. The adversary has no power over me, but all power over all the power of the enemy has been given unto me by the Lord Jesus Christ. I live inside Your hedge. I live and rejoice in my redemption, which was purchased for me at Calvary. I will stay inside Your hedge. I will keep my shield of faith intact, and*

*I will use my weapon. Thank you, Lord, that all of the
enemy's fiery darts are quenched.*

If you have made holes in your hedge by running back
and forth through it, if you have not used the sword of the
Spirit, if you have received the attacks of the enemy, *do not
get under condemnation.* The time when you are wounded
is no time to allow the enemy to bring condemnation on
you as another fiery dart!

Learning such truths as God is revealing about His
Word in this book is the place where you begin to live the
Christian life. If you already were walking in total victory,
you might not need to be reading and learning.

So if you are in the process of having your faith built
by hearing the Word, then find a good church where you
can hear more and more of the Word, find people to get
in agreement with you to "shore up" your hedge, and most
of all, get in the Word of God. Make it an entire way of
life. Read it out loud to yourself, and your hedge will
become more and more secure.

6

Fear Makes Holes in Your Hedge

Thou shalt not be afraid for the terror by night;
nor for the arrow that flieth by day;

Nor for the pestilence that walketh in darkness;
nor for the destruction that wasteth at noonday.

A thousand shall fall at thy side,
and ten thousand at thy right hand;
but it shall not come nigh thee.

Psalm 91:5-7

There are four more things about Job's situation that I want you to look at, because they will help you to better understand Psalm 91 under the New Covenant. Those things are:

1. God placed a hedge around Job.

2. This hedge looked like a great fence to Satan.

3. God narrowed the perimeter of that fence to include only Job's life.

4. Job's fear about losing his children and his possessions may have been what ultimately gave the devil access to them. On the other hand, Job was *not* afraid of losing his life, so his being in agreement with God in this area allowed God to preserve his life. First, look at the verses that show fear.

> **And it was so, when the days of their** (Job's sons' and daughters') **feasting were gone about, that Job sent and sanctified them, and rose up early in the morning, and offered burnt offerings according to the number of them all: for Job said, It may be that my sons have**

57

sinned, and cursed God in their hearts. Thus did Job continually. (He *feared* for his children.)

Job 1:5

For the thing which I *greatly feared* is come upon me, and that which I was afraid of is come unto me.

I was not in safety, neither had I rest, neither was I quiet; yet trouble came.

Job 3:25,26

Another translation of those two verses says:[1]

For a fear I feared and it meeteth me, And what I was afraid of doth come to me. I was not safe — nor was I quiet — nor was I at rest — and trouble cometh!

Now, let's look at the verse that shows Job was *not* in fear over losing his life.

For I know that my redeemer liveth, and that he shall stand at the latter day upon the earth:

And though after my skin worms destroy this body, yet in my flesh shall I see God:

Whom I shall see for myself, and mine eyes shall behold, and not another; though my reins be consumed within me.

Job 19:25-27

For years those verses have driven liberal theologians up the wall. People in Job's day were not supposed to know about the Redeemer. They did not have the New Covenant. They were not supposed to have an understanding of the Messiah. Not until the New Testament is it spelled out clearly in writing by inspiration of the Holy Spirit that when Jesus returns for His Body, we will see God in the flesh.

Yet Job anticipated seeing God. He understood that he was going to stand before God when he died. He understood that he was going to live on, so he was not afraid

---

[1]Young, Robert. *Young's Literal Translation of the Holy Bible,* Revised Edition (Grand Rapids: Baker Book House, 1898, Third Edition), p. 338.

of dying. The one thing Job did *not* fear was physical death. He was afraid he would lose his money, he was afraid his children would die and all his cattle, he was afraid a storm would come and blow away his house, but he was not afraid of losing his life.

Because he feared all of those things, however, he was *stepping outside the hedge.*

Jesus addressed a similar situation in Matthew 23:37, when He said:

> **O Jerusalem, Jerusalem, thou that killest the prophets, and stonest them which are sent unto thee, how often would I have gathered thy children together, even as a hen gathereth her chickens under her wings, and ye would not!**

What Jesus actually was saying is this:

"Listen, Jerusalem, you have gotten outside the hedge. You stepped outside the fence. Everytime a prophet comes, you kill him. You have stoned the prophets. Everyone who tries to tell you to get back behind the fence, you kill.

"How often would I have gathered you as a hen gathers her little chicks beneath her wings, but you would not let Me. I would have brought you back inside the hedge, but because you would not allow it, your house is left unto you desolate. Because you got outside my protection, Satan is going to come in and wipe out your city and your nation."

Thou Shalt Not Be Afraid

If you are not to be afraid in the daytime, or the nighttime, in the light or in the darkness, then when can you be afraid? The answer is that God has not made any provision for His children to be afraid at *any* time. He did not leave out one minute of the night or day. He did not leave out any place you can go on the face of the earth and have an excuse to be afraid.

59

That statement is not a platitude or a phrase injected to fill space. *It is a commandment.* The reason Psalm 91 does not work for many Christians is that they never get beyond that commandment. However, it is *more* than a commandment, it is a prophetic statement.

When all of the things in the first four verses are working in your life, when the secret place of the Most High is a reality to you, *then* you shall not be afraid. If you are covered with His feathers and trusting in His wings, you will not fear.

That is a pretty good indicator that when fear grips us, we have not been walking in the light of our redemption. When you find that fear has come into your life, when you are constantly battling fear, you are not living in the provisions of Psalm 91.

There are two kinds of people who deal with fear. Those in the first group believe fear is something they already have and are trying to get rid of. Those in the second group believe that fear belongs to Satan, who is trying to put it on them. Which group are you in?

Members of the first group would say, "I have a lot of fears in my life. There are a lot of things that 'scare me to death.' "

Members of the second group say, "I used to have fear, because Satan is full of fears. Now I am a new creature in Christ Jesus, and all of the old things in my nature have passed away. All things have become new. I do not have any fear, but Satan tries to put his fears on me. And I am not going to receive any fear."

Romans 8:15 tells you the truth about fear:

> **For ye have not received the spirit of bondage again to fear: But ye have received the Spirit of adoption, whereby we cry, Abba, Father.**

If you have received the spirit of adoption, then obviously you do not have a spirit of bondage. The spirit that brings bondage brings fear. God did not give us fear. He gave us power, love, and a sound mind. *Fear does not come from God.*

We are told to "fear" God, but that means "to reverence" God, to bow down and worship God. We are to be in awe of the Creator of the universe and everything in it. But when He is our Father, we do not *fear* Him in the sense of "terror and panic."

Another way of looking at the attitude of fear and what it causes is this:

Those in the first group of people, who have fear and are trying to get rid of it, have reverence *for what they fear*. The latest allergy, losing their jobs, all kinds of problems — those are what they spend time thinking and talking about. They "bow down" to their fears, while those in the second group bow down to God. Your heavenly Father does not want you bowing down to anything but Him.

Fearing anything will result in your bowing down to it. You reverence it. "Bowing down" is not only an act of worship, but it is an act of submission. You can bow down to the Father in voluntary submission and not be in bondage. *But you cannot bow down to anything else in the world without coming under bondage to it.*

Psalm 91:5 says you will not be afraid of the terror at night. *Terror* also means "dread," so you will not dread the darkness or be afraid of the dark. If you are afraid, it always gets worse at night. Have you noticed that? If you are sick, most of the time, it seems you get worse at night. There apparently is a very close connection between this matter of fear and your physical health.

There is something about fear and darkness and night that seems to cause them to flow together. Somehow if you have fear, you feel more vulnerable in the dark and at night. However, Satan really does not care whether it is dark or not; he wants to bring destruction even in the noon day.

Men's Hearts Fail for Fear

The prophetic verse of Luke 21:25 says that men's hearts will fail them for fear because of looking at the things that are coming on the earth, **for the powers of heaven shall be shaken.**

I was not born until long after the Great Depression of 1929. Yet, some thirty years later, when I was young, many people were in fear of another one — "We may have another depression. What if we have another depression?" When I was a child, most adults remembered those awful times, or had heard of them from their parents so much that it seemed they remembered.

They were afraid the same things could happen again. Then we went through the period when everyone was afraid of nuclear war. Now the world also is fearing environmental destruction of one kind or another. Men's hearts probably have failed them for fear more in this century than any since Christ.

But none of these "fears" can equal all of the signs in the sun, moon, and stars that Jesus said were going to happen in the future. Worldwide, at that time, many men will have hearts failing them for fear. When all of those things begin to happen in the sky, it is going to be quite awesome.

A lot of Christians have their hearts turned toward problems in natural circumstances, and if things began to happen in the universe right now, their hearts would fail them for fear. Their hearts are built up and ready for fear, not for trust in God.

What is the cure for this? The cure is to get your heart and attention back on the Word of God. The cure is to take the position God takes: not to allow fear to become part of your life at any time nor in any place.

You may say, "Oh, but I just can't help it."

Verses 1-4 of Psalm 91 tell you how to help it. They tell you how to reach that place of safety, how to be in the position of escape. Another psalm sheds more light on this:

> **My soul is among lions: and I lie even among them that are set on fire, even the sons of men, whose teeth are spears and arrows, and their tongue a sharp sword.**
>
> **Psalm 57:4**

The Apostle Peter wrote that the devil "walks about as a roaring lion" looking for those believers that he can devour. (1 Pet. 5:8.) *Which* believers? Satan seeks to devour those who do not **resist stedfast in the faith** (v. 9).

Men Are Not Your Enemies

The author of Psalm 57 refers to men who come against you along with the devil. But what the psalmist really was talking about is the enemy working *through* men.

Remember that any time someone says something bad about you, anytime someone criticizes you, complains about something you have done, disagrees with you, or even curses you — *do not get angry*. Satan is taking advantage of weaknesses in that person to strike out at the weaknesses in you.

Love your enemy. Love those who despitefully use you. Love is a choice, not a feeling. Make a decision to love them with the love of Jesus, and that will put the brakes on Satan's ability to work through that person to strike out at you.

So, in Psalm 57, the composer is really talking about Satan working through men to shoot fiery darts. The devil or any of his demons can only speak to your mind. He cannot speak to you audibly, which is why he uses human voices to reach your natural ear.

He works through those who will receive his thoughts and act on them. Satan taunts and works in an individual's life, a person who is susceptible because of certain thoughts of his own, and stirs him up so that he becomes a voice for the enemy.

Several other scriptures along this line may come to your mind. One that comes to my mind is Isaiah 54:17:

> **No weapon that is formed against thee shall prosper, and every tongue that shall rise against thee in judgment thou shalt condemn. . . .**

No matter what it is, the Holy Spirit said under the Old Covenant — and we have a *better* one — no weapon formed against the people of God shall prosper. Some of the weapons the devil has formed against us are poverty, sickness and disease, rejection and persecution, and fear.

Then He assured us that anyone who rises up against us will be condemned in judgment. That does not mean to rise up and say to those people, "I condemn you." What the Holy Spirit was saying is for us to take a firm stand in God's Word. Then we will come out on top, and everyone who was listening to those things that were said will see that you were the one who rose to the top. The person saying all those things was the one who was wrong.

Isaiah 54:17 ends this way:

> **. . . This is the heritage of the servants of the Lord, and their righteousness is of me.**

Isaiah 43:1 says:

> **Fear not: for I have redeemed thee.**

If fear becomes a real part of your life, you are not walking in the light of your redemption.

> **. . . Fear not: for I have redeemed thee, I have called thee by thy name; thou art mine.**
>
> **When thou passest through the waters, I will be with thee; and through the rivers, they shall not overflow thee: when thou walkest through the fire, thou shalt not be burned; neither shall the flame kindle upon thee.**

For I am the Lord thy God, the Holy One of Israel, thy Saviour. . . .

Isaiah 43:1-3

Under the New Covenant, the Apostle John put it this way:

There is *no fear in love;* but perfect love casteth out fear: because fear hath torment. He that feareth is not made perfect in love.

1 John 4:18

7

Faith Works by Love

A thousand shall fall at thy side,
and ten thousand at thy right hand;
but it shall not come nigh thee.

Psalm 91:7

Now we come to verse 7 of Psalm 91. This is the verse that has caused it to be called "the serviceman's psalm." That promise sounds wonderful. But how can a thousand fall at your side and ten thousand at your right hand?

First of all, remember that in Deuteronomy 32:30,31, we saw that the rock of our enemies is Satan. Our Rock is the Lord Jesus Christ. Their rock "sells them out," and our rock shuts them up. Who is *them*? They are all of the enemy shooting the arrows that fly by day, bringing the pestilence in the darkness, and causing the destruction that wastes at noonday.

The "thousand at your side" and the "ten thousand at your right hand" are those of Satan's host that would come against you. You see the Word is saying that if you will remain, stay, or *live* in the shadow of the Almighty, you shall not fear.

You will not fear because no matter how many demons come against you, no matter how many people are out there working against you and running their mouths all day long against you, just stand firm in the Lord, and He will shut them up. You will see a thousand fall at your side.

In Deuteronomy 32:30, Moses told us a little more about how this can come about. He shows that if even two believers get in agreement, they can put ten thousand to flight instead of a thousand.

When you understand all of the ramifications of what these verses really mean, then *thou shalt not be afraid* stops being an impersonal commandment and becomes a reality.

You can say, "I don't have fear that I'm trying to get rid of. No! Fear will not come near me. Satan will not put that fear on me."

And if the fear does not come on you, then Satan cannot put the wasting, the pestilence, and the destruction on you, either. In the words of the prophet Isaiah:

No weapon that is formed against thee shall prosper.

Isaiah 54:17a

Many times, when people get ready to take a trip, they want to pray, "Oh, Lord, keep us safe. Oh, Lord, protect us. Oh, Lord, go with us."

Even when it comes to traveling, if you will go with Him and dwell in the secret place of the Most High, you will abide under the shadow of the Almighty, and accidents or mishaps will not come near you.

Incorporate this truth into your life. Take it everywhere you go. Make living in the Word a lifestyle, and you will not fear.

I am sure that you noticed a difference in expression between what was said in Deuteronomy 32:30 and Psalm 91:7.

Moses wrote about "chasing" and "putting to flight," and the psalmist wrote about thousands "falling." You might say that the enemies of God's people were going to run and then fall, but I think there is more to it than that.

Whatever it is that is going to run or fall, whoever is going to be put to flight, it is not supposed to be born-again, Spirit-filled, Word-believing people!

Believers Are Not To Be Put To Flight

There have been times when I have seen two Christians trying to "outbelieve" one another. Perhaps you have never seen two Spirit-filled Christians both believing for the same thing. But I certainly have. In one instance, there was a building for sale in a certain city, and each of two men was "believing God" and "confessing" that the building was his.

These two men knew each other very well. Neither of them would give in. I suppose each thought his faith was stronger, so God would honor his believing over the other man's. What kind of position does that put God in? Both of them forgot that *faith works by love.*

God never intended for me to use my faith against another believer. God never intended for us to believe for another brother in Christ to run or fall. He never intended for us to try to outdo or outwit one another.

Under the Old Covenant, God worked in behalf of Israel. He caused a lot of people to run from them and be defeated. However, those who were defeated were unbelievers allowing themselves to be used by the devil against God's people.

In spite of how it looks in the Old Testament in the natural, God was never coming against the people but defeating the enemy working through them. The people always had the choice of cooperating with Israel or working against her. And, if they were not for God, they were for Satan and were used by him.

Consider Rahab in Jericho just before Israel began to march around the walls. (Josh. 2.) If she recognized God in what was happening and chose to come over on His side, thus saving her entire family, it stands to reason there were others who could have done the same.

In Joshua 9, the inhabitants of Gibeon came over on the side of the Lord by making a treaty with Israel, thus escaping destruction.

Some Christians today who work with people who are interfering with what they want, begin to believe God to do something to those individuals. I have heard some pretty strong "faith confessions" concerning what God was going to do about some other person who was in that believer's way. All of that is based on a misunderstanding of the Word.

People are never your problem. It is a mistake to begin to look at the person causing trouble and not see the enemy behind that person. God was never coming against the people. The reason those people were run over and killed was because they allowed themselves to become instruments of Satan.

I am not talking about demon possession. I am simply talking about people who allow Satan to work through them. When anyone complains, grumbles, gossips, criticizes, and judges, he is being an instrument of Satan as much as when he covets, lusts, steals, or commits adultery.

When a person allows Satan to cause him to walk in doubt and lack of trust, he is being an instrument of the devil. You may think worry and doubt are not sins, but the Word says, **for whatsoever is not of faith is sin** (Rom. 14:23b). That is a very strong statement that Christians like to overlook!

People do not often quote that, but they say, "I know I'm not in faith like I ought to be; I'm not believing God like I ought to, I'm not walking in faith like I ought to. I'm doubting the promises in God's Word."

They do not think this is sin. They have this little "problem." The truth is that they do not believe God's Word.

This is not meant as condemnation, but to give you understanding. Perhaps this is an area you have not seen before. But if you allow yourself to get caught up with complaining and criticizing other people, or your pastor and leaders of your church, you are allowing Satan to use you to some degree as one of his instruments.

We must watch ourselves and keep ourselves in line with God's Word, so that at no time do we become an instrument through which Satan is able to do some of his work.

God Does Not Want Any To Perish

Satan is destined to run. Satan is destined to fall. Satan is destined to be destroyed. If he is working in you and through you, then when he runs, *you are going to run*. When he gets knocked down, you will too. Those thousands of people in the Old Testament who were destroyed had so aligned themselves with the enemy that when he ran or fell, so did they.

One example that is proof of the fact that God did not want any of them to die is the city of Nineveh. This was a whole city that had become instruments of Satan. The devil had full and complete right of way in their lives to do anything he wanted to, but God still did not want them to be destroyed.

So He sent a little Hebrew man over there to warn them to repent. (Jonah 1-4.) God had a hard time getting Jonah there. Why was Jonah reluctant to go preach to Nineveh? He was not afraid, but the Assyrians were so wicked that Jonah did not want them to be saved!

> **And God saw their works, that they turned from their evil way; and God repented of the evil, that he had said that he would do unto them; and he did it not.**
>
> **But it displeased Jonah exceedingly, and he was very angry.**

71

> And he prayed unto the Lord, and said, I pray
> thee, O Lord, was not this my saying, when I was yet
> in my country? Therefore I fled before unto Tarshish:
> for I knew that thou art a gracious God, and merciful,
> slow to anger, and of great kindness, and repentest
> thee of the evil.

> Jonah 3:10–4:2

In other words, Jonah said, "Lord, I knew you were loving and kind and hard to provoke. I told you this is what You would do! I knew You would save them if they repented, and they deserve to be destroyed!"

God got the situation changed, and those people were no longer instruments of Satan. The whole city was saved.

Also, look at Sodom and Gomorrah. An entire city had become the instruments of Satan in terms of sexual perversion, self-indulgence, and violence against one another. In spite of that, God began to look for an intercessor so He would not have to destroy them.

He went to Abraham, who began to pray that God spare the city for at least 50 righteous. God agreed, and Abraham began a countdown to 10. But there he stopped. He must have assumed there were at least that many righteous in his nephew Lot's household. But he was wrong.

What if he had kept going to three, or even one? God did not want the city destroyed, although the people allowed Satan to work through them all day and all night, apparently. God did not want those people destroyed, but neither did he want Satan to be able to use them to contaminate or destroy Abraham's seed.

That is what was happening with Moses and Pharaoh, as well. The Egyptians of that time had become instruments of Satan. They were cruel and mean. The Bible says they were hard taskmasters. (Exod. 1:8-14.) God did His best to separate those people from being instruments of Satan. He must have known the demonic powers were headed for the bottom of the Red Sea, and if the people would not be separated from them, that is where they would end up as well.

Because Satan was working through them, the Egyptians had become enemies of God's people. If Pharaoh had said, "Okay, I believe your God is the real, true God. He is Lord," Bible history would read a lot differently.

Remember the story of the demon-possessed man of Gadara who ran out of the tombs at Jesus? When Jesus cast the demons out of him, they entered into pigs and the pigs ran into the water. If Pharaoh had committed to believe in God, the nation would have followed him, and Israel would have left Egypt. I think all of those demonic forces that had been working through the Egyptians might still have wound up at the bottom of the Red Sea.

This is similar to what will happen at the Great White Throne judgment. (Rev. 20:11.) God never intended for a single human being to go to hell. He did not prepare hell for humans. (Matt. 25:41.) He has done everything within His power, short of overriding man's inherent right to choose, to keep human beings out of hell.

God sent His only Son, Jesus, to be crucified because He loved human beings, His creation, so much. (John 3:16.) It is not His will for any to perish. (2 Pet. 3:9.)

But Satan and all of his forces are headed that way, fast and furiously. When Satan goes to hell, those who have aligned themselves with him will go along, in spite of God's love and the way to escape He has prepared.

God Always Wins

God always wins.

God always comes out on top.

God never fails.

God never runs.

God always is successful.

If you are God's instrument, if He is working in and through you, and if you are inseparable from Him, then *when He wins, you win!*

When He stands strong, you stand strong.

When a thousand fall at His side, they fall at your side.

Are you seeing the underlying principle here? *Satan always is going to lose.* He is always going to wind up on the bottom. It does not make any difference what you think is going on in the world, or how successful someone looks who is not living for God, Satan is always going to lose. So are his instruments. They may not "lose" until they die, but they are losers.

Every human being is a "born loser" until he or she is *born again*. Then those people become "born winners."

Situations and circumstances in the world may look as if God lost, but He did not. The humans involved who were Satan's instruments are the ones who lost.

Suppose on your job, you decide, "Well, if I really want things to change, I had better raise some racket around here."

Then you begin to criticize, use sharp words, cause hurt feelings, and misuse a few people, because, "If you just step on a few people around here, you'll get someone's attention. Then they will do something for you."

Even if you achieve your objective, you have lost, because you allowed Satan to use you as his instrument. What happened to the fact that God is love? What happened to the truth that God is love, and that love works by faith?

On the other hand, if you become an instrument of God, and stay in line with His Word, you will come out on top in the end.

If you are aligned with God, then the last statement in Psalm 91:7 will come true: **it shall not come nigh thee.**

When Mr. Believer understands that in dealing with Mr. Unbeliever, he is dealing with the god that lives in that person, then Mr. Believer can deal with the situation according to the God whom he serves, the Almighty. Sometimes, unfortunately, another believer still acts as though he is serving the enemy. To that extent, Satan will use that person as an instrument.

I have met quite a few believers who did not walk according to the principles of the Word. They tried to walk all over me. They misused and mistreated me and said horrible things about me. I *wanted* to react to the person, but I did not say a word. I knew who my enemy really was, and it was not those people. If I had reacted, I would have been following his ways the same as those who were attacking me. I would have been no better an instrument of God than they.

A good example of this is Jesus at His trial. Why did He not yell out at those men heckling and tormenting Him? Why did He not answer His accusers? Why did He not respond? Those men thought they were attacking Jesus when they hung Him on a cross until He died.

However, Jesus knew they were coming against the Father and not Him. He knew the God inside of Him was ultimately bigger than all of them. He knew what was really coming against Him was all the forces of hell working in and through those men.

He did not bother to answer. Anything He could have said had already been said during His three years of ministry. Also, He knew that God always wins. Three days later, He arose from the dead. Who won? God or Satan? Those men or Jesus?

Believers need to be aware that anytime they are being attacked, if they will stay in the Word of God and operate in love, they cannot be defeated. If they begin to react to people or circumstances, then they begin to allow Satan to operate through them — and they will lose, because he always loses.

Psalm 91:7 will work for you when you have identified yourself with God, because **greater is he that is in you, than he that is in the world** (1 John 4:4).

You may think this is too simple. You may say, "Well, if it is all God and Satan, then where do human beings fit into all this?"

We are the only ones who can choose.

Satan cannot choose for you. He cannot make the decision that you are to be his instrument. He cannot decide that you are going to fail, be destroyed, or cast down. He does not have the right, privilege, or ability to make choices for you.

Neither will God make choices for you. Of course, He is sovereign. He can *do* anything. However, His whole plan for mankind is based on allowing each individual the *right to choose*. If He were going to choose for man, He would choose for each person to be saved. That is His will; however, each person has the right to choose God's will for his life, or to choose his own way — which really is Satan's way.

A lot of Christians say, "Oh, I don't know about all of this. I see things happening in other people's lives, and I see destruction here and destruction there, and I get concerned. After all, if it happens to them, who am I?"

I have just been telling you who you are. You are the person who is aligned with the One Who always wins. Your God always stands and never fails. He will never fall. I believe that, even if your house is on a certain street and a tornado strikes, your house will be left standing.

Many times, we spiritualize the promises entirely. We want to think this psalm only means demons cannot come near us. However, the more your life is aligned with the Word of God, you will come to the place of looking back at the people you have known for the past 10 or 20 years and seeing how one, then another, has fallen.

You will hear how this one has that problem, and the other had this problem. All the while, you have walked right through the middle of things, and life has been beautiful. You will look at people you went to school with several years ago, and they look 20 years older than you do, although they are the same age as you.

You will hear of this one having a heart attack, and that one going into a rest home. And here you are just as strong, going right on, and enjoying life.

Why? I repeat one more time that it is certainly not because God wants them to fall or to fail. You have won, and they have been losers because you chose to abide under the shadow of the Almighty. God has been winning all those years in and through your life, and you have won along with Him.

Psalm 91:7 begins for you with a decision. Go back and look at some of the stories in the Old Testament. You will see that when Israel was aligned with her God, the nation won. When they lost, it was because they had forsaken God and aligned themselves with the enemy.

I know my God, and I know His book, so I can tell you with certainty that God had a plan for Israel to occupy the Promised Land without a single one of them being killed. The central theme of the whole Bible is that God is not willing that any should perish, but that all should come to repentance.

He gave His only begotten Son to *defeat the works of Satan* (John 3:16; 1 John 3:8), and those works were defeated at Calvary.

When Israel finally marched into the Promised Land, their story had spread all over the region:

"This is a group of people whose God has brought them out of slavery in Egypt. They are extremely wealthy and blessed. Their God even parted the Red Sea for them to walk over on dry land. He provided food for them supernaturally and water out of a rock."

When they reached Canaan, the first people they came to should have opened their arms and said, "Come on in and tell us about your God." That was God's plan.

Why did things not work out that way? Israel would not make the decision to walk totally in alignment with God. They kept getting into disobedience and rebellion, which caused them to become instruments of Satan. Those who yielded to the temptation, doubt, and fear of the enemy lost when he lost. They died in the wilderness.

However, God won. His plan for defeating the works of Satan and having a people who would love Him *by choice* and walk in His ways *by choice* kept right on going into effect.

If you have allowed yourself to become aligned with Satan in any way, all you have to do is repent and come back to the Winner. Align your life with God's will and way — obey His Word, listen to the still, small voice of the Holy Spirit, and you will become a winner. You will be able to live that victorious life many people talk and preach about and many others yearn for.

8

Satan's Three Basic Tactics Temptation, Doubt, and Fear

*Only with thine eyes shalt thou behold
and see the reward of the wicked.*

*Because thou hast made the Lord,
which is my refuge, even the most High
thy habitation;*

*There shall no evil befall thee,
neither shall any plague come nigh
thy dwelling.*

Psalm 91:8-10

Look at verse 8 in the light of what we have learned about verses 5-7:

We are not to be afraid for:
- The terror by night,
- The arrow by day,
- The pestilence in the darkness,
- The destruction at noon.

You are not to fear those things because a thousand are falling at your side and ten thousand at your right hand, *but whatever it is will not come near you.*

Verse 8 continues the thought. You will see those things, but they will not touch you.

You are not to be afraid of any kind of terror at night, *because it will not come near you.*

You are not to be afraid of the arrow (something that comes to kill) by day, *because it will not touch you.*

You are not to be afraid of pestilence (sickness and disease), *because it cannot come near you.*

You are not to be afraid of any kind of destruction, *because poverty, tornadoes, floods, and so forth, cannot come near your dwelling.*

Even if a thousand people drop dead at your side and ten thousand all around you, you are not to fear. You will still be standing.

It is the wicked who will be terrified at night, hit by arrows, destroyed by pestilence. Satan has no positive emotions regarding those who serve him. Fear, hatred, and brute force (power) in the supernatural demonic realm are what governs the attitudes of Satan toward his cohorts, and among them, to one another.

So he certainly has no feelings for the people he deceives or tempts into serving him. He does not care how many people he kills, makes sick, or destroys. The more the better, as far as he is concerned. He knows now for sure that he cannot defeat God. All that is left is for him to take as many humans with him as he can and to delay the accomplishing of God's plan as long as He can.

Satan uses three basic tactics to get men to work with him: temptation, doubt, and fear. He also has three basic lies through which he presents these tactics.

Three Basic Lies

Satan's three basic lies are:

1. "Everyone else is doing it, why don't you?" This is an insidious thought of the enemy that leads you into *temptation.*

2. "If it is not working for anyone else, why do you think God's Word will work for you?" This thought builds *doubt* instead of faith.

3. "Terror, pestilence, and destruction are happening to other people. I see those things all around me. Why

shouldn't it happen to me as well?'' Of course, that idea is *fear*.

If you will understand these lies, and get them firmly fixed in your mind *as lies*, then the next time one of these thoughts comes to you, you will know the enemy is speaking.

If you are not very alert, lie number three can slip into your thinking easily. Because there are so many believers who do not yet know how to walk in faith, it is easy to line up a long list of born-again people who have gotten the flu, or cancer, or have had their houses broken into. Before you know it, you are believing the lie that it is happening to everyone else; therefore, it is also going to happen to you.

That is exactly what Satan wants. He creates this cycle over and over again, using those three basic lies. If you will examine your own life, you will find that a large percentage of the time when you were defeated, one of those three lies was involved.

Satan loves to point out people and speak these thoughts to your mind: ''See, that scripture didn't work for them. They didn't get healed. They didn't get the money they needed. What makes you think you're going to?''

He ignores, and you overlook, that those people may not have believed they were going to get their prayers answered in the first place. You can count on the fact that those people had fallen for one of Satan's basic three lies, or they would have been victorious.

Satan knows that certain things cannot be *proven* in the natural, and he keeps working this edge against us. He will scare, terrify, mutilate, destroy, cause plague after plague, and anything else he can do to shake our belief in God.

What God wants you to realize is that some of His children find out how to abide under the shelter of His wings and some do not. Be one of those who do. Believe the Word of God and not the words of Satan.

For example, Satan may try to convince you that one out of four people gets cancer, so you will get it. Just remember that, in that case, three out of four will not get it. You determine to be one of those who do not, because Jesus is your hedge against the pestilence.

If you believed one scripture that you could be born again (Rom. 10:9,10), and it happened, and you believed another scripture that you could be filled with the Spirit (Mark 16:17, 1 Cor. 14:2,4,14), and it happened, why would Psalm 91 not be true as well?

When you take hold of this one little verse, **it shall not come nigh thee** (Ps. 91:7b), I promise you that you will live a successful Christian life. Meet the conditions of dwelling in the secret place of the Most High, and you are qualified for that kind of protection. You will see the works of Satan, but they will not come near you.

Live by Faith, Not Sight

Human beings tend to think that anything they can see is more real than what they cannot see. I cannot see the shadow of the Almighty. I have never seen the "feathers and wings" the psalmist wrote about. *But I have seen the wicked destroyed.* I have seen the reward of the wicked. I have beheld thousands and ten thousands falling.

I remember the polio scare when I was a child. Everyone was afraid of polio. I can still vividly recall waking up one morning with a headache and checking to see if I also had a stiff neck!

We saw a lot of people with polio, and those iron lungs that many of them had to live in made quite an impression. You would look at that and be terrified. That was so real! If something like that is rampant in our society — as AIDS is now — it can become more real to you than the shadow of the Almighty.

Not only that, we have the tendency to think that anything we see *is* nigh us. We relate *close* with *nigh*. Something that is far away from us, we think, is something we cannot see with our natural eyes. And, if something is close enough to see, we feel it is close enough to "get" us.

But, the Holy Spirit said through the psalmist that we would see it, and yet, it would not come near us. (v. 7,8.)

I do not know how far your physical eyes can see, but I have been in an airplane on a clear day when you could see for miles and miles. Another plane could be close enough for me to see, but that did not mean it would come near us.

Satan can only get within a certain distance of my refuge. He can get only so close to my habitation. As long as I stay in my dwelling, Satan and his plagues and evil cannot come nigh me. And this is a *big* habitation I am talking about. I can look out the windows and see what he is doing to thousands of people around, and he can see me looking out at him. However, he cannot do those things to me.

The only way Satan can get close enough to me to do me any harm is for me to move closer to him. I can leave my habitation, and be vulnerable to his attacks.

Really, it does not take a lot of "gray matter" to figure out which is the best thing to do. But Satan keeps telling you lies. He catches you looking out the window and says, "Look what's happening to all those people!"

God will do everything He can to keep you from leaving His habitation. He will not force you to stay inside, but He will give you warning after warning not to go outside of His protection. His warnings are kind, gentle signals in your spirit. That "check" you feel now and then is God trying to keep you from harm.

I remember a time in my Christian life when I had just started getting hold of the Word in my heart. I would have a few days that were just great.

And I would think, "Man! Living for God is the greatest thing in the world. This is tremendous. Everything is going great."

Then I would kind of get out of the Word. Things would begin to happen. I would have a few problems come along, and I would struggle with them for a few weeks. Then I would get back in the Word, overcome the problems, and climb back up on top of the pile again.

I was up and down, up and down. Finally, one day I decided that if I could just level off and stay somewhere between up and down, that would be pretty good. I kept feeding my spirit the Word of God. Then I remember the first time I went for days and days and days without a problem. Nothing went wrong. Nothing bad happened. I began to think something was wrong because nothing was wrong!

I had come to *expect* that what I was seeing happen to other people was going to happen to me. Later, I began to see that expectation was very wrong. I came to see I had no right to expect things to happen to me that happen to the unrighteous.

Now, I do not *expect* to get sick. I do not *expect* problems. I do not anticipate turmoil, strife, sickness, and disease. When my wife and I plan trips, we expect to have a beautiful time. Nothing is going to go wrong. Why? Because as we travel, we are going to dwell in the secret place of the Most High and abide under the shadow of the Almighty.

No matter what comes nigh other people, it will not come nigh me. I believe that, and as I grow in faith, I am finding plenty of good things to put my faith on, and plenty of good things to believe are going to happen to me. I do not waste my faith on believing negative things.

I am going to state this fact of the Word very strongly: *A Christian has no right to expect all the horrible things to happen to him that happen to people in the world.*

We could turn to the New Testament and look at scripture after scripture that say the same thing in different words. One of those is 1 Peter 2:24: **By whose** (Jesus) **stripes ye were healed.** That points out the boundary line God drew with the blood of Jesus.

God said, "I'm drawing the line right here, Satan, and you can't cross that line."

Every person who is born again stepped across the line and got on the side where the Father is. But so many of them do not know they have crossed that line, so they keep stepping back across the line and picking up Satan's sicknesses and diseases.

But when God drew that line, you *were* healed. That means if you are born again and living on God's side of that line, He never intends for you to be sick again. As far as God is concerned, it is over. But every now and then, one of us will slip out of the habitation of God. The things of Satan still do not come nigh us, but we come nigh them.

At this point, if you are one of those who keeps slipping out of the secret place of the Most High, you need to stop and take a look at your life. You need to seek God on what causes you to move over that line. What is it that happens causing you to come nigh those things of Satan's? Because it certainly is not that he is able to cross the blood of Jesus to get near to you.

Once you became a righteous person, when any of Satan's junk gets near you, it is because *you* got near *it*.

What every Christian needs to do is simply look at his or her own life daily, and make sure to stay in the secret place of the Most High. Tell yourself this every day:

Today, I am going to abide under the shadow of the Almighty. And tomorrow, all day long I am going to make sure I abide under the shadow of the Almighty.

9

The Role of Angels
in the New Covenant

**For He shall give his angels charge over thee,
to keep thee in all thy ways.**

**They shall bear thee up in their hands,
lest thou dash thy foot against a stone.**

Psalm 91:11,12

Verse 11 actually refers back to verse 10. If you used *because* instead of *For* in verse 11, it would be more obvious.

"No evil will happen to you, and no plague will come near your house, *because* God has angels watching over you."

Then the psalmist went on to write, under the inspiration of the Holy Spirit, that the angels would carry him so that he would not even hit his foot against a rock. From those three verses, 10-12, we can see that angels have a lot to do with the lives of God's children.

Many evil things, plagues, even accidents, do not occur in believers' lives because of angels. In the last few years, a lot has been taught and written about angels. It has been as though the Church just awakened in modern times to the fact that angels do exist and have a purpose and reason for existence.

Of course, most of us have always known that angels really exist, but there has been a tremendous amount of uncertainty concerning their purpose and reason for being.

I grew up thinking God made angels just to praise Him, and that was all they ever did.

I thought there was one large group of angels who all had wings and who just stood praising God year after year, century after century. All the other angels were little fat babies with bows and arrows. That was my concept of angelic beings.

Then I began to see that angels were very, very active under the Old Covenant, and I also saw them in the New Testament.

As far as we are concerned today, I suppose the favorite scripture about angels is Hebrews 13:2:

> **Be not forgetful to entertain strangers: for thereby some have entertained angels unawares.**

I hear that scripture used in reference to angels more than any other. Often, the underlying interpretation is that if angels have anything to do with your life, you will probably never know it.

Until I began to study the Word of God for myself concerning angels, I did not learn a whole lot more about the subject. In fact, it seemed that the only things attributed to angels were things for which we had no other explanation!

In the next two chapters, I want to share some things the Lord has taught me from His Word about angels.

Seven Conclusions About Angels

In the New Testament, one verse often referred to about angels is Matthew 18:10:

> **Take heed that ye despise not one of these little ones; for I say unto you, That in heaven their angels do always behold the face of my Father which is in heaven.**

When we consider Psalm 37:4, Matthew 18:10, and Psalm 91:10-12, there are several things that immediately become obvious:

1. When we are born, or as children, angels are assigned to us. We can draw that conclusion immediately. In Matthew 18:2, the apostle writes about Jesus drawing a little child to Him. Then He set that child in the midst of them and began to teach the disciples. Verse 10, quoted above, is in the context of that teaching.

2. When Jesus said the angels of **these little ones...do always behold the face of My Father which is in heaven,** that means the angels always have immediate access to the presence of God the Father.

3. We know the Word of God is true; therefore, that means there are a lot of angels right here on this earth. Yet the Word says they have immediate access to the Father in heaven. That tells you something very comforting about angels, if you stop and think a minute.

An angel who is standing right beside you this minute can be before the throne of God in less than a split second. Imagine! He can be standing in the very visible presence of the Father, facing the throne, and then be back with you the very next second.

4. There is a definite purpose connected with each angel's assignment which must be related to terms of protection. Jesus said, **Take heed that ye despise not one of these little ones.** That is a warning.

Jesus had this little child in front of a group of people. In essence, He was saying:

"Angels are assigned to these little ones for their protection. You had better be very careful about despising one of these little ones, because there are angels who have immediate access to the presence of the Father, angels personally assigned to these little ones to protect them. So if you decide that you are going to despise and come against them, look out!"

5. The angels are assigned to the little ones, and encamp around about those who fear God.

6. The angels deliver those who fear God. (Ps. 34:7.)

7. The angels deliver those who dwell in the secret place from evil and plagues. They keep us in all our ways and bear us up in their hands, not even allowing us to dash our feet against a stone.

Those are seven basic assumptions, or conclusions, that you can arrive at based on just the few scriptures I have shared.

Another conclusion we can draw is that Satan is aware of these facts I have just shared. We know that because it was Psalm 91:11,12 that Satan quoted to Jesus during the time He was tempting him.

The Devil Even Distorts the Bible

Compare Matthew 4:5,6; Luke 4:9-11; and, Psalm 91:11,12:

> Then the devil taketh him up into the holy city, and setteth him on a pinnacle of the temple,
>
> And saith unto him, If thou be the Son of God, cast thyself down: for it is written, He shall give his angels charge concerning thee: and in their hands they shall bear thee up, *lest at any time* thou dash thy foot against a stone.
>
> **Matthew 4:5,6**
>
> And he brought him to Jerusalem, and set him on a pinnacle of the temple, and said unto him, If thou be the Son of God, cast thyself down from hence:
>
> For it is written, He shall give his angels charge over thee, to keep thee:

And in their hands they shall bear thee up, *lest at any time* thou dash thy foot against a stone.

Luke 4:9-11

For he shall give his angels charge over thee, to keep thee in all thy ways.

They shall bear thee up in their hands, lest thou dash thy foot against a stone.

Psalm 91:11,12

As you compare Matthew 4 with Luke 4, you see there is a difference in the wording, but the thought remains the same. However, in both Matthew 4:6 and Luke 4:10,11, the devil used almost exactly the same wording. But did he quote Psalm 91:11 and 12 correctly?

No, he did not quote it correctly. He misquoted the passage by inserting four words, **lest at any time.** The 91st Psalm does not say, "at any time." It says, *when you dwell in the secret place of the Most High.*

The devil cannot even quote scriptures correctly. The Word says he is a liar and the father of lies. The truth is not in him. (John 8:44.) He not only could not quote the verse right, he had to add something to make his quote a lie, not truth.

Jesus knew that yielding to Satan in any way would be ceasing to dwell in the secret place of the Most High. Jesus knew when He went into the wilderness that He was going to be tempted by Satan. And He knew that yielding to that temptation would cause him to come out of the secret place of the Most High.

Also, Jesus knew the Word of God, and He knew that the devil had misquoted the Word. Jesus could not deliberately get out of the Word and expect angels to protect Him. Satan was taking the chance that Jesus did not know the Old Testament, and if He had not known it, He *might* have been tricked.

91

He could have said, "Well, the devil is quoting one of David's psalms, but even if he is the enemy, the Word is true. So, if I jump off this pinnacle, the angels are going to be there because the Father said it."

Satan also takes that chance with you. You will find that the more of God's Word you know, the easier it will be to refuse temptation. You will know from the Word some things so definitely that Satan will never try to tempt you with those things again. He will not waste his time.

That would be like the devil telling Jesus, "See that bread? You are tired and hungry. Steal that bread and eat it. Your Father will forgive you. He understands where you are. He will overlook it this one time."

That would have been so clear cut, so obviously wrong, that it would not even have been a temptation. But the devil tests Jesus' knowledge of the Word by adding one little wrong phrase.

This is not legalism; however, *we are responsible for what we know.* If you know the Word, the devil cannot fool you with misquotes from the Bible, so that you get into presumption instead of faith.

God's Grace Is Infinite

Because of God's grace, there are times when angels intervene for people who are *not* dwelling in the secret place of the Most High. However, to deliberately, knowingly not dwell in that place, and yet expect to count on angelic protection is not only foolish, but presumptuous.

A fellow I know was in Vietnam during the war. One day, he was assigned to transport supplies from one position to another in one of those large helicopters. All day long, he and the crew flew back and forth delivering supplies from one spot to another.

This young man was not a Christian at the time. He knew nothing about the Lord Jesus. Furthermore, he was taking all the drugs he could get his hands on and drinking all the beer he could get. And he was getting plenty of both, according to him.

They had not seen any Vietcong all day. There had not been any shots fired at them until sunset, when they were on the way back to the base after making the last trip. As they flew over the jungle, suddenly there was a loud explosion, and the helicopter blew apart. There were five men on this mission, I believe, and all of them were killed but this young man.

He told me he was lying on the floor of the helicopter, and the next thing he knew, he was standing in the middle of a field completely unharmed, with not even a scratch or bruise. The helicopter was about 1,500 feet away going up in flames, and the other men who were with him were dead.

How did he get in that field? That was the grace of God in operation. My friend definitely was *not* dwelling in the secret place of the Most High. He did not even have the right to hope that God would send an angel to get him out of that helicopter and away from the flames without a scratch or bruise.

I have to believe there was an angel who had something to do with that. Now, this young man is born again, filled with the Spirit, and so is his wife. The last time I saw them, both were serving God and being great witnesses for the Lord Jesus. There are many stories like that. Evidently the angels have saved the lives of countless humans who did not know God.

People will say, "When I was in sin, when I did not know Jesus, this or that happened to me — and I know it must have been an angel."

That is God's sovereign grace, and the angels acted for God's reasons. However, you cannot count on that always happening. The one thing you *can* count on is what God has promised in His Word: If you live under the shadow of the Almighty, you can *expect* the angels to be there when you need them.

Moving Closer to Angels

Angels are not born again. They were not created in the image of God, and they do not have the right to choose. Jesus did not die for angels. All angels were already set in their places long before Jesus came to earth as a baby.

Those who chose illegally to go with Satan were cast out of heaven. Those who remained in the "first estate," the place and position where they were placed by God are still in their places. Those angels dwell in the secret place of the Most High, in the shadow of the Almighty, but in a different sense than we do.

They are there because God created them to be there, and they were obedient. We are there because of our redemption by Jesus *and our own choices*. We can stay there because Jesus died for us, was buried, and rose again, and we have believed in our hearts and confessed with our mouths that Jesus Christ is Lord.

Angels who are in the secret place of God now are not about to leave it. They have seen the results of rebellion. So when we move into that place, we are not only moving closer to God, we are moving closer to His angels. And they encamp around those who fear the Lord.

Not only would the enemy have to get past the hedge of our redemption, he would have to get past that wall of angels! I have never seen an angel that I know of, but I have heard other people tell of seeing angels. If angels look anything like what I have heard described, I know the enemy is never going to get past them. But the main reason I know he will not get past them is because the Word says so.

The Word states very clearly that the enemy will not come near my dwelling because angels are encamped around me. They do not just hang around there a few hours a day. They are not there today and off on vacation next week. They are there all of the time.

God is concerned about the very smallest thing that happens to you. We are as one with Him, so anything affecting our lives is very definitely having an effect upon God, and everything going on with God is very definitely having an impact on our lives.

The smartest thing you can do as a Christian is move closer and closer to God. Get inside that secret place, and live there.

10

In Charge of Angels

He shall give his angels charge over thee.

Psalm 91:11a

To shed some more light on the role of angels, let's look at Numbers 22:

> And the children of Israel set forward, and pitched in the plains of Moab on this side Jordan by Jericho.
>
> And Balak the son of Zippor saw all that Israel had done to the Amorites.
>
> And Moab was sore afraid of the people, because they were many: and Moab was distressed because of the children of Israel.
>
> And Moab said unto the elders of Midian, Now shall this company lick up all that are round about us, as the ox licketh up the grass of the field. And Balak the son of Zippor was king of the Moabites at that time.

Numbers 22:1-4

Balak was afraid of the people of Israel. Why was he afraid? He was afraid they could do to his nation what they had done to the Amorites. He was afraid the Israelites were going to move in and completely take over, because there were so many of them.

He used the figure of speech that they would "lick up everything around just as an ox licks up the grass of the field." He actually was afraid that Israel would use up all of the food supply, and the nation of Moab would be

97

overrun. So he made a decision to do something about it, something that would give Moab an "edge" over Israel.

> **He sent messengers therefore unto Balaam the son of Beor to Pethor, which is by the river of the land of the children of his people, to call him, saying, Behold, there is a people come out from Egypt: behold, they cover the face of the earth, and they abide over against me:**

> **Come now therefore, I pray thee, curse me this people; for they are too mighty for me: peradventure I shall prevail, that we may smite them, and that I may drive them out of the land: for I wot that he whom thou blessest is blessed, and he whom thou cursest is cursed.**

> **Numbers 22:5,6**

Balaam apparently was noted for the fact that his blessings and cursings came true. He was not a false prophet. He was not a witch or warlock. He was a godly man, who talked to the true God about what he did.

The elders of Moab and the elders of Midian came together and made a trip to Balaam's house with money of some kind to pay for his efforts on their behalf. They told Balaam what the king wanted him to do, and the prophet asked them to spend the night while he talked to the Lord about the situation.

> **And God came unto Balaam, and said, What men are these with thee?**

> **And Balaam said unto God, Balak the son of Zippor, king of Moab, hath sent unto me, saying,** (and he told God who the men were and what the king had sent them for — as if God did not already know!) . . . .

> **And God said unto Balaam, Thou shalt not go with them; thou shalt not curse the people: for they are blessed.**

> **Numbers 22:9,10,12**

The next morning, Balaam told the delegation that God had forbidden him to curse this people. They went back and told the king, who immediately tried again. This time, he sent a higher level delegation and promised Balaam not only riches but great honor. In fact, the king told Balaam he could "write his own ticket," ask whatever he chose.

And Balaam answered and said unto the servants of Balak, If Balak would give me his house full of silver and gold, I cannot go beyond the word of the Lord my God, to do less or more.

Numbers 22:18

But that night, he approached the Lord again:

And God came unto Balaam at night, and said unto him, *If the men come to call thee,* rise up, and go with them; but yet the word which I shall say unto thee, that shalt thou do.

And Balaam rose up in the morning, and saddled his ass, and went with the princes of Moab.

And God's anger was kindled because he went: and the angel of the Lord stood in the way for an adversary against him.

Verses 18,20-22a

Why was God's anger kindled? Evidently Balaam did not do what God had said to do. The Lord told him that *if* the men called him, he was to go and speak only what God said. Balaam was "pulling on God's coat tail" like a whining child begging for his own way. God patiently gave him a sign to watch for, an indication of His will, as well as having told him not to go in the first place.

An Angel Stops a Prophet

Balaam did not wait to be called by the men. He rose up, saddled his donkey, and took off. As he and his two servants rode along, an angel stood in the way with his sword drawn. The donkey saw the angel and turned out of the road into a field. But Balaam hit the animal a good hard lick to turn her back onto the path.

> **But the angel of the Lord stood in a path of the vineyards, a wall being on this side, and a wall on that side.**
>
> **And when the ass saw the angel of the Lord, she thrust herself unto the wall, and crushed Balaam's foot against the wall: and he smote her again.**
>
> **And the angel of the Lord went further, and stood in a narrow place, where was no way to turn either to the right hand or to the left.**
>
> **And when the ass saw the angel of the Lord, she fell down under Balaam: and Balaam's anger was kindled, and he smote the ass with a staff.**
>
> **And the Lord opened the mouth of the ass, and she said unto Balaam, What have I done unto thee, that thou hast smitten me these three times?**
>
> **And Balaam said unto the ass, Because thou hast mocked me: I would there were a sword in mine hand, for now would I kill thee.**
>
> **Numbers 22:24-29**

Apparently Balaam was so enraged that he did not think it strange for his donkey to speak to him, because he answered her! Anyone who has ever worked with donkeys can surely understand Balaam's feelings.

One summer when I was just into my teens, I had a friend whose uncle owned an amusement park, and the fourth of July was coming up. He had several little donkeys for children to ride at the park. The donkeys were kept in a short corral with fences on each side.

The children were put on at one end of the corral and rode around the fence to get off at the other end. I took a job helping for the fourth of July. I had never been around a donkey in my life. If I had read this Bible story before then, I might have been wiser.

However, I kind of know how Balaam felt! Every time the fireworks went off, so did the donkeys. I would be at one end of the corral, and some fireworks would go off, and all of a sudden, the donkeys would be back down at the other end with the little kids hanging on for dear life.

That was quite an experience, so I do have some sympathy for Balaam. At the time his donkey spoke, he had not yet seen the angel. But he had ridden this animal, and he knew her personality! Apparently, he thought his donkey was just being herself. About that time, however, the Lord opened his eyes, and he saw the angel with a drawn sword.

Balaam did the first smart thing he had done all morning: he bowed his head and fell on his face. And the angel scolded him sternly, telling Balaam the donkey had saved his life. If she had not seen the angel and had ridden on into him, Balaam would have died! (vv. 31-33.)

So the prophet repented and offered to turn back home. (v. 34.)

> **And the angel of the Lord said unto Balaam, Go with the men: but only the word that I shall speak unto thee, that thou shalt speak. So Balaam went with the princes of Balak.**
>
> **Numbers 22:35**

The story goes on and on, because Balaam was very, very persistent about getting his own way — in spite of the warnings from God. In fact, three times, Balak made a very serious attempt to get the prophet to curse Israel, and Balaam tried every way he could think of to get around God's prohibition.

The Lord knew the temptation to curse Israel was going to grow stronger and stronger, and He took strong measures to help Balaam resist the temptation. In the end, Balaam did find a way around God's instructions — not to curse

Israel directly but to help Balak and the Moab-Midian coalition.

Numbers 31:16 says that he advised Balak to use Moabite women to seduce the Israelite men, and a plague fell on Israel because of this. Then, when the next generation of Israel finally marched into the Promised Land, Joshua 13:22 tells us that Balaam was among those slain by the sword.

In spite of God's speaking to Balaam Himself and then sending His angel to warn him, the prophet is mentioned throughout the New Testament for his sin, which was prostituting the gifts of God for personal gain. (2 Pet. 2:15, Jude 11, and Rev. 2:14.)

The point is that angels worked with God's people under the Old Covenant, but angels cannot cause men's hearts to change. Only Jesus through the New Covenant can do that.

The thing I like best about this story is that it shows so well the extent to which God will go to keep one of His children from making a mess out of his life. Balaam did not set out to defy God, or he would have gone with the first delegation. His heart was toward God, but the lust of the world sparked disobedience.

An Angel Saves an Apostle

Now let us look at a very different story. This one is found in Acts 12.

> Now about that time Herod the king stretched forth his hands to vex certain of the church.
>
> And he killed James the brother of John with the sword.
>
> And because he saw it pleased the Jews, he proceeded further to take Peter also. (Then were the days of unleavened bread.)

And when he had apprehended him, he put him
in prison, and delivered him to four quaternions of
soldiers to keep him; intending after Easter to bring
him forth to the people.

Peter therefore was kept in prison, but prayer was
made without ceasing of the church unto God for him.

And when Herod would have brought him forth,
the same night Peter was sleeping between two
soldiers, bound with two chains: and the keepers
before the door kept the prison.

And, behold, the angel of the Lord came upon
him, and a light shined in the prison: and he smote
Peter on the side, and raised him up, saying, Arise up
quickly. And his chains fell off from his hands.

And the angel said unto him, Gird thyself, and
bind on thy sandals. And so he did. And he saith unto
him, Cast thy garment about thee, and follow me.

And he went out, and followed him; and wist not
that it was true which was done by the angel; but
thought he saw a vision.

Acts 12:1-9

Up to a certain point, Balaam did not know there was
an angel in front of him. Some odd things were going on,
such as his donkey speaking to him, but he had not seen
the angel.

In Peter's case, he also saw some very interesting things
happening, but at first he did not realize what was
happening was real. He was sound asleep, the soldiers were
beside him, his chains fell off, the guards were outside the
door, and he followed an angel out of the door. However,
he was still half-asleep and thought all of that was a vision.

When they were past the first and the second
ward, they came unto the iron gate that leadeth unto
the city; which opened to them of his own accord: and
they went out, and passed on through one street; and
forthwith the angel departed from him.

And when Peter was come to himself, he said, Now I know of a surety, that the Lord hath sent his angel, and hath delivered me out of the hand of Herod, and from all the expectation of the people of the Jews.

And when he had considered the thing, he came to the house of Mary the mother of John, whose surname was Mark; where many were gathered together praying.

And as Peter knocked at the door of the gate, a damsel came to hearken, named Rhoda.

And when she knew Peter's voice, she opened not the gate for gladness, but ran in, and told how Peter stood before the gate.

And they said unto her, Thou art mad. But she constantly affirmed that it was even so. (Many Christians operate this same way: pray earnestly, but then would doubt it was true if their prayers were answered!) **Then said, they, It is his angel.**

But Peter continued knocking: and when they had opened the door, and saw him, they were astonished.

Acts 12:10-16

The thing I want you to see in this story is that an *angel was given charge* over Peter's safety. And I want you to see the difference between an angel being given charge over someone in the Old Testament and someone in the New Testament.

Balaam was about to get into something that would put him in opposition to the will of God. He was on the verge of making a mistake. As we saw earlier, in the end, Balaam moved into disobedience. But, in the beginning of this incident, when Balak tried three times to get him to curse Israel, Balaam in fact blessed them three times.

The angel of the Lord was sent to Balaam to keep him from making a mistake. Hopefully, he would take heed to the message of the angel and not be disobedient.

104

In the case of Peter, who was in trouble for *obeying* the Lord, the angel was sent to rescue him *and to keep Herod from making a mistake.*

The angel saved Peter from being killed by Herod. Peter not only got out of prison but was able to go his way preaching the Word of God.

Angels Make a Hedge

The Hebrew word translated *charge* in Psalm 91:11 is *taavah,* which means "to enjoin, to appoint," or "to send with."[1] So the Lord was saying He would appoint or send angels with the one who dwells in His secret place. The angels sent to Balaam and to Peter carried out their assignments and then apparently went on to do something else.

Also, the New Testament saints apparently had some understanding of this, because they thought the maidservant had seen Peter's angel. The assumption was that Peter had a personal angel.

Verse 11 then says that angels are appointed to keep us in all our ways. The Hebrew word translated *keep* is *shamar* which means "to hedge about (as with thorns), i.e. guard; to protect, to attend to, etc." Also, it can mean "to observe, to preserve," or "to watch."[2] So, the angels are appointed to form a hedge about us, to guard, protect, and observe us, in order that they may preserve us.

You need to understand, however, that angels do not control our lives. They do not determine our activities. They do not keep us from sinning. The direction of your life is *your* responsibility. For angels to do their jobs, for them to fulfill the commissions they have been given, we must abide under the shadow of the Almighty.

---

[1]Strong. "Hebrew and Chaldee Dictionary," p. 98.
[2]Ibid, p. 118.

We should not be trying to figure out how far we can go and still have angelic protection. It seems there always are people wanting to do that. That is not the point. The point is to stay close to the Lord. If we do what we are supposed to do, the angels can do what *they* are supposed to do, and we will be protected.

Verse 12 says the angels **shall bear thee up.** The Hebrew word for *bear* used in verse 12 is *nacah*, a root word that has many meanings, among which are "to lift," "to spare," and "to raise (up)."[3]

When I began to study this verse, I wondered if there was an illustration I could use that would clarify the phrase, **bear thee up in their hands.** So I began to study the Hebrew word *kaph* used for *hands.* I found this is not the usual word used for hand or hands. This word refers to the *palm* of the hand, or for the "bowl of a dish or sling . . . the leaves of a palm tree."[4]

When I saw that, I thought of hands cupped together. If you were real small and being held in the hands of a giant, there would be what amounted to a hedge around you. And this is the picture being presented in this verse.

The Hebrew word used for *dash* in **lest thou dash** (v. 12) is used only that one time in the Old Testament. The word is *nagaph*, which has a variety of meanings, anything from "stub (the toe)" to being pushed, gored as by a bull, defeated, hurt, plagued, or struck in any way. The last definition in *Strong's New Exhaustive Concordance* is to "put to the worse!"[5]

So you might read that phrase as "lest you be put to the worse." When the devil tempted Jesus and quoted this

---

[3]Ibid, p. 81.
[4]Ibid, p. 57.
[5]Ibid, p. 76, #5062.

verse in the New Testament (Matt. 4:6, Luke 4:11), the Greek word is *proskopto*, which means the same thing as the Hebrew.[6]

You can see that God simply found another way to express the same sentiment as in **no evil shall befall thee** (v. 10) and:

> **A thousand shall fall at thy side, and ten thousand at thy right hand; but it shall not come nigh thee.**
>
> **Psalm 91:7**

There is a tremendous amount of repetition in Psalm 91, not repetition of words, but repetition of meanings:

- **The secret place of the Most High** (v. 1).
- **The shadow of the Almighty** (v. 1).
- **He is my refuge and my fortress** (v. 2).
- **Deliver thee from the snare of the fowler** (v. 3).
- **He shall cover thee with his feathers** (v. 4).
- **His truth shall be thy shield and buckler** (v. 4).
- **The Lord . . . thy habitation** (v. 9).
- **He shall give his angels charge over thee** (v. 11).

And there are other phrases in this psalm that we have not yet talked about that reiterate the same idea. The Holy Spirit was trying to drive home to the hearts of those who heard or read this psalm that there is a place in God where there is safety from the enemy.

---

[6]Strong. "Greek Dictionary of the New Testament," p. 61, #4350.

11

What Is Underneath Our Feet?

**Thou shalt tread upon the lion and adder:
the young lion and the dragon shalt thou
trample under feet.**

Psalm 91:13

Most of this book has been spent discussing what is above us and around us. Now it is time to talk about what is underneath our feet.

Like the rest of Psalm 91, the promises are future tense: Thou *shalt*. Many of the psalms are prophetic. Psalm 91 is prophetic in the sense that, until Jesus was crucified and rose from the dead, the children of God were not able to walk in the fullness of these promises.

Of course, you know that you are not literally to go out and walk on lions or snakes and expect to be protected! One cult in the Appalachian Mountains has gotten way out in left field by taking such expressions literally. In fact, we are dealing with figures of speech throughout the entire 91st psalm. God *really* does not have feathers!

The dictionary definition of *figure of speech* is: "Using words in a nonliteral sense or unusual manner to add vividness, beauty, etc. to what is said or written."[1]

The Hebrew language is rich in such colorful figures of speech, expressions that add illumination to the concept they represent. The concepts or things represented by these

---

[1]*Webster's New World Dictionary*, 3rd Coll. Ed., s. v. "figure of speech."

figures of speech are literally true, although the words themselves are not literal.

So we know God does not have feathers, but that expression gives us a comforting knowledge that He will gather us under His protection *just as* a mother hen gathers her chickens under her wings. That expression tells us that God loves us, wants to protect us, and that in Him there is safety.

Somehow that mental picture of a mother hen and chickens (which Jesus used of Jerusalem in Matt. 23:37) is graphic and real to us. The promise in a mental picture explains more to us than simply saying, ''If you stay in the Word of God and close to Him in your daily walk and prayer life, He will protect you.''

The expressions used were used everyday in David's time and were easily understood by his people. However, this 13th verse would be meaningless to most of us if it were literal. Most of us never see lions except in a zoo, and many Christians have never encountered a poisonous snake.

Figures of Speech Paint Real Pictures

When I was a teenager, I very foolishly stomped a snake to death. I did not have anything in my hands to hit it with, and I had on shoes. He was there, and I was there, and he did not seem to want to go the way I wanted him to go — away! So I jumped on him with both feet and literally trampled him to death.

I know now that was dangerous, because a rattlesnake's fangs can pierce even heavy boots. I have had no other occasion to be faced with that kind of situation. Also, I do not plan to do it again!

However, this verse was not talking about real lions and snakes, but about a time when Satan and his demons would be placed beneath our feet. That is why I say this verse, in particular, is prophetic.

This promise is one of the earliest in the Bible. God spoke it in a prophecy to the serpent, Satan, but it was for the hope of mankind.

And the Lord God said unto the serpent, Because thou hast done this, thou art cursed above all cattle, and above every beast of the field; upon thy belly shalt thou go, and dust shalt thou eat all the days of thy life.

And I will put enmity between thee and the woman, and between thy seed and her seed; it shall bruise thy head, and thou shalt bruise his heel.

Genesis 3:14,15

When David wrote Psalm 91, Satan was not beneath his feet. David could dwell in the secret place of the Most High, and he could receive many of the other promises in that psalm. But he could not tread on Satan. The devil still had the dominion over the earth that he got illegally from Adam and Eve.

The devil *was* a heel bruiser — but he is not that anymore; at least, not to God's children. However, we can see from what God said to him, **upon thy belly shalt thou go,** that He intended all of the time for us to put Satan under our feet. That is why He put him on his belly, eating dust. He put Satan under the feet of mankind at the very moment the devil thought he had won dominion over the earth forever.

Now look at Luke 10:18,19:

And he said unto them, I beheld Satan as lightning fall from heaven.

Behold, I give unto you power to tread on serpents and scorpions, and over all the power of the enemy: and nothing shall by any means hurt you.

Psalm 91:13 is not prophetic any longer. It has been fulfilled. Jesus defeated the serpent, Satan, and He will yet punish the devil and all of his demons by casting them into the lake of fire. (Rev. 20:10.)

111

The context of Luke 10 shows that Jesus was not speaking literally anymore than the psalmist had been. He really was using a figure of speech to tell the disciples that Satan had been put under their feet in a spiritual sense.

However, as Jesus continued to talk, He put matters in the proper perspective:

> **Notwithstanding in this rejoice not, that the spirits are subject unto you; but rather rejoice, because your names are written in heaven.**
>
> **Luke 10:20**

How could Jesus give us that power? In the first place, He could delegate His power to us after His resurrection because God the Father put everything under the feet of Jesus. First Corinthians 15:27 says, **For he** (God) **hath put all things under his** (Jesus') **feet.**

Jesus was given all power over Satan by the Father, and then Jesus delegated that power to the Church, His Body, individually and corporately. Of course, "all things," means everything but God. (1 Cor. 15:21,28.)

All Things Are Under Our Feet

Look at Paul's letter to the church at Ephesus:

> **The eyes of your understanding being enlightened; that ye may know what is the hope of his calling, and what the riches of the glory of his inheritance in the saints,**
>
> **And what is the exceeding greatness of his power to usward who believe, according to the working of his mighty power.**
>
> **Which he wrought in Christ, when he raised him from the dead, and set him at his own right hand in the heavenly places,**
>
> **Far above all principality, and power, and might, and dominion, and every name that is named, not only in this world, but also in that which is to come:**

And *hath put all things under his feet,* and gave him to be the head over all things to the church,

Which is his body, the fulness of him that filleth all in all.

Ephesians 1:18-23

And you hath he quickened, who were dead in trespasses and sins;

Wherein in time past ye walked according to the course of this world, according to the prince of the power of the air, the spirit that now worketh in the children of disobedience:

Among whom also we all had our conversation (citizenship) in times past in the lusts of our flesh, fulfilling the desires of the flesh and of the mind; and were by nature the children of wrath, even as others.

But God, who is rich in mercy, for his great love wherewith he loved us,

Even when we were dead in sins, hath quickened us together with Christ, (by grace ye are saved;)

And hath raised us up together, and made us sit together in heavenly places in Christ Jesus:

That in the ages to come he might shew the exceeding riches of his grace in his kindness toward us through Christ Jesus.

Ephesians 2:1-7

When God raised Jesus from the dead, He raised us with Him. When were you raised from the dead? Not the day you were born again. That is the day you *received* having been raised from the dead. That is when you accepted the fact that new life was yours the moment you confessed Jesus Christ as your Lord and Savior.

But God the Father *saw* you raised from the dead when He raised Jesus. He saw every person who would ever be born again made spiritually alive when Jesus was

113

resurrected. Not last week, nor last month, nor last year, but almost 2,000 years ago, God raised all of us up together with Jesus.

When He set Jesus at His own right hand, God also set us in heavenly places in Christ Jesus. This happened in God's mind and sight that very instant. So, if you were raised up with Jesus and all things were put under your feet, then where are you now?

Jesus knew the moment He sat down in heavenly places at the right hand of the Father that His power over the enemy would belong to every man and woman who believed on Him. He knew that moment, thank God, that we could tread on "serpents" and "scorpions." So He said, **Behold, I give unto you power . . . and nothing shall by any means hurt you** (Luke 10:19).

But that is not the end of the story.

The Rest of the Story

Look at Hebrews 2:

For unto the angels hath he not put in subjection the world to come, whereof we speak.

But one in a certain place testified, saying, What is man, that thou art mindful of him? or the son of man, that thou visitest him? (Ps. 8:4.)

Thou madest him (man) a little lower than the angels; thou crownedst him with glory and honour, and didst set him (man, in the Garden of Eden) over the works of thy hands: (Ps. 8:5,6.)

Thou hast put *all things in subjection under his feet.* For in that he put all in subjection under him, he left nothing that is not put under him. But now we see not yet all things put under him (man).

Hebrews 2:5-8

In the next verse, the writer of Hebrews switches from writing about man to writing about Jesus specifically.

114

But we see Jesus, **who was made a little lower than the angels** (took on the nature of man) **for the suffering of death, crowned with glory and honour; that he by the grace of God should taste death for every man.**

Hebrews 2:9

As the seed of Adam, we were a little lower than the angels, and when Jesus came as man under the Old Covenant, he was also made a little lower than the angels, as we see in the verses above.

However, the end of the story is found in Hebrews 1, where the writer pointed out that God used to speak to His people through prophets, but from now on would speak by His Son, Jesus, by Whom He made the worlds and Who had been appointed heir of all things. Then he wrote:

Who being the brightness of his glory, and the express image of his person, and upholding all things by the word of his power, when he had by himself purged our sins, sat down on the right hand of the Majesty on high:

Being made so much better than the angels, **as he hath by inheritance obtained a more excellent name than they.**

For unto which of the angels said he at any time, Thou art my Son, this day have I begotten thee? And again, I will be to him a Father, and he shall be to me a Son?

And again, when he bringeth in the first begotten into the world, he saith, And let all the angels of God worship him.

And of the angels he saith, Who maketh his angels spirits, and his ministers a flame of fire.

But unto the Son he saith, Thy throne, O God, is for ever and ever: a sceptre of righteousness is the sceptre of thy kingdom.

Hebrews 1:3-8

As joint heirs with Jesus, and as new creatures through Him, we also have been made "better" than angels. And part of our inheritance through Jesus will be putting death — the last enemy — under our feet. The last enemy is physical death. Spiritual death, which came on Adam and Eve when they sinned, was immediately put under foot at Calvary.

Jesus has already suffered death and has been crowned with glory and honor. Thank God, we can have *eternal* life right this moment. Our physical bodies are going to die, but the moment we are loosed from these physical bodies, we enter into a complete and total forever-life with the Lord Jesus.

The death of the physical body is no problem, because **to be absent from the body,** is **to be present with the Lord** (2 Cor. 5:8b). Jesus could give us that right, because we have been raised up with Him, far above all principalities and powers.

We can tread on the adder. We can "trample" demons under our feet. Satan is not even a heel bruiser anymore, because Jesus said, **Nothing shall by any means hurt you** (Luke 10:19). Jesus has put all things under subjection to us except physical death, and that is ours by His provision, although the manifestation will not come until the Resurrection.

Keep the enemy, Satan, under your feet where he belongs. Stop seeing him in front of the window, shooting arrows in at you. If you understand that he is under your feet, you can move any way God tells you to move. You do not have to be hesitant in following God's leading. You do not have to fear doing the will of God when you know that every step you take in obedience to the Father means you are trampling the enemy under your feet.

When Christians are afraid to do what the Word of God says, it is because in their minds they have allowed the enemy to slip out from under their feet and get out in front of them. Then all they can see is him. Keep him under your feet. That is where God intends for him to be. That is the reason He raised you up with the Lord Jesus.

Do not let demons sit on your shoulder and whisper to you. They have no business there *at all*. Yank them off your shoulder and step on them!

You do not have to wait until Jesus returns to have victory over the enemy. You will not need to trample him underfoot during the Millennium or after. He will be bound in prison for 1,000 years and then thrown into the lake of fire. (Rev. 20:1-7.)

God is not talking about something to happen some day. In the New Testament, the Holy Spirit inspired the writers to tell of something that already has occurred and that Christians of the past almost-2,000 years have had a right to appropriate.

Satan Is Down

If you are not walking the Christian life with the devil under your feet, probably it is because you have not known this is the position in which God wanted you to be. I used to let the devil run me around all the time, because I did not know these things. Many Christians still have no comprehension of their position in relation to the enemy.

If Satan has been giving you a rough time, your understanding of his position *and* yours needs to be enlightened. The quicker you get hold of the truth that Satan is down and you are up, the more victory you are going to have. Also, that understanding will cause your life in Jesus to become better, your praying more effective, and your mind more peaceable.

Psalm 91:13 says: **Thou** *shalt* **tread upon the lion and the adder.** That is not only future tense but is a command.

David uttered those words in a prophetic sense, but today, they have been fulfilled. They are a reality right now, if you will just learn to walk in that reality instead of Satan's delusion that he is powerful and you are not.

But why did David write that we would tread on the lion *and* the young lion? When I first looked at that, I wondered about it. Obviously, the words are not just a repetition for emphasis, because the second reference to lion has an adjective — the descriptive word *young* — added.

When I began to study this, I saw that a young lion is a *roaring* lion. Older lions tend not to roar as much. Someone has said that the mark of immaturity is a big mouth. People who are spiritually mature have quiet spirits and the ability to keep their mouths shut.

More mature people are quieter because they have learned to bridle their tongues. But the devil has the biggest mouth of anything in existence! Why? That is because he is the least spiritually mature. First Peter 5:8,9 explains this very well:

> **Be sober, be vigilant, because your adversary the devil, as a roaring lion, walketh about, seeking whom he may devour.**
>
> **Whom resist stedfast in the faith, knowing that the same afflictions are accomplished in your brethren that are in the world.**

How do you resist the devil and see him flee from you? Which way does he flee? I used to picture this as him out in front of me, and when I would speak the Word to him, he would run away from me. Then I remembered that Jesus told the devil to get behind Him. (Luke 4:8.) Then I saw the devil running off behind me.

However, when Jesus spoke to the devil, He had not yet put him underfoot. From the time of Jesus' resurrection on, Satan has been under our feet. He has to go down. He cannot go any other way. So I trample on him. You may ask how to trample on the devil. You do it with the Word of God.

When you read Ephesians 6 concerning putting on the full armor of God, you see that our feet are to be shod with the preparation of the Gospel of peace. Thank God for that. Maintain peace in your heart, and you will resist the enemy. You speak the Word, and you will drive him farther, farther, and farther down.

Down is the only direction God has intended Satan to go from the time he rebelled and was thrown out of heaven. The devil *walks* about seeking whom he may devour, and the eyes of the Lord *run* to and fro. (Zech. 4:10.) So if the eyes of the Lord are running, and the devil is walking, there is no way the devil can get to you before the Lord does.

The downfall of Satan runs from Genesis to Revelation, and so does the raising up of Jesus, our Blessed Hope.

12

Set Your Love Upon God

Because he hath set his love upon me,
therefore will I deliver him:
I will set him on high,
because he hath known my name.

He shall call upon me, and I will answer him:
I will be with him in trouble;
I will deliver him, and honour him.

With long life will I satisfy him,
and shew him my salvation.

Psalm 91:14-16

These three verses mark a change in this psalm, which really should be divided into two parts, because it has two different speakers. Part one, verses 1-13, is the psalmist, generally considered to be David, talking about the Lord and what it means to live in the shadow of His wings.

Verses 14-16 are God speaking to the psalmist, in the first person. God said, "The person who sets his love on Me, I:

- Will deliver."
- Will set on high."
- Will answer."
- Will be with in trouble."
- Will honour."
- Will satisfy with long life."

Notice also that for the very first time in this psalm, the word *love* is mentioned. God made an unequivocal

121

statement, leaving absolutely no room for question: He *will* deliver those who establish their love on Him.

The word *set* in verse 14 means "fixed." Sometimes it seems that when we tell people they need to love God, or love one another, our words come out kind of like, "All you have to do is nothing. All you need is some kind of feeling."

But God was not talking about a feeling, or a passing fancy, or something nice that occurs once in a while.

He was saying, "Because you have determined, no matter what, that you love Me, then nothing will come before Me in your heart. You have fixed your love on Me to the exclusion of family, career, friends, ministry, and even life."

That is a "quality decision."

Also, God did not say, "I will deliver him because I have set My love on him."

God set His love on us, His creation, before the beginning of time. He established that love on record in the universe forever when He sent the Lord Jesus to die for us at Calvary. God has set His love on man eternally.

However, the fact that will bring you deliverance is that *you* set *your* love on God.

God longs to deliver man, but what enables Him to fulfill this longing is man's response to what God *already* has done. Man needs to set his love upon God. When you set your love on God, that gives Him the spiritually legal right, the opportunity, the opening to deliver you.

You will always find that the deliverance God is able to bring to a man's life is determined by the degree to which he has set his love upon God.

Jesus said for us to love God with our heart, soul, mind, and strength. (Mark 12:30.) There are Christians who love God with their hearts, but their minds are set on something else. God has delivered their hearts through salvation, but their minds are filled with the world.

Then there are people who do not love God with their bodies. They let their bodies do as they please, although their hearts love God. Setting all of their love on God, without holding back any area, will bring deliverance in all areas.

Satan Wants To Hold Us Hostage

When the Iran hostage crisis was going on during the late-Seventies, the Lord showed me something about the devil and his operations.

The assumptions the Iranian government were operating on were these:

— Because the hostages are American citizens, the rest of us have set our love on them.

— Because they are American citizens, they have set their love on their country.

— *Therefore,* we would ransom them out of bondage in any way the kidnappers asked *because we love them and they love us.* The whole world was watching, and if the United States did not deliver its people from this situation, then that would have shown that the country did not care about its citizens.

Then some of the hostages were forced to make public statements criticizing their country. Iran was walking a fine line with all of this, and the scheme followed the devil's tactics. Of course, that was because the whole idea of it came from him to the Ayatollah Khomeini.

Satan holds the majority of mankind as hostages and has been doing that since Adam and Eve were put out of the Garden of Eden.

Why did Satan come to Eve in the first place? His temptation of Adam and Eve was not because the devil cared anything about man. He had no desire for the human race. But he had lost his own place with God. He had been dethroned and lost his power. He had not only lost his position, he had lost everything.

So he set out to take man hostage, because he saw that *God had set his love* on mankind. No doubt he thought, and perhaps still thinks, that because God loves us and we love God, that he will be able to get what he wants out of God.

Perhaps he thought in the very beginning, "I'll just take the whole thing hostage, and I will be able to force God into giving me what I want. I will get God to do for me what I want."

He still wants even more authority than he used to have before he was kicked out of heaven. Satan set out to hold mankind hostage. No doubt, he still thinks by striking back at God in this way, he can get what he wants.

But God sent Jesus to die for you and me to establish that He has the legal right to get His hostages away from the devil. The only thing that is now necessary to get away from the one who holds you captive is for you to receive Jesus as the ransom payment.

Satan, however, has always done what the Ayatollah did: attempt to brainwash the hostages to get them to make humiliating and derogatory statements about God. He thinks that is "publicly" embarrassing God. He sets Christians up in various problem situations or actual destruction, thinking their plights will cause others to wonder whether God really loves His children.

He wants us to wonder whether God's Word is true and whether He really will deliver us. The truth, of course, is that God *already has* delivered us. Now it is up to us to receive that deliverance.

God said to David, "Everytime I see a man held hostage by the devil, a man who has set his love on Me, I will deliver him" — and He has.

The Sign of Love Set on God

A way has been established in which God could absolutely tell that a man had set his love upon the Most High. Of course God knows our hearts; however, in Psalm 91:14, God gave a sign of an established heart, one that is *set* on God. That sign is found in the last phrase of that verse. The Lord said, *because he hath known my name.*

In Romans 10:9, God said that if you believe in your heart and confess with your mouth that Jesus was raised from the dead, you will be saved. And you cannot do that without setting your love upon God. The moment you make that confession and receive Jesus as Lord, immediately God has the legal right to deliver you. You are no longer Satan's hostage.

God is saying, therefore, in Psalm 91:14, "I am going to establish the one who sets his love on me in such a way that he is secure because he has known My name."

In ancient times, names had real meaning. A person's name made a statement about him or her. Today, names are simply labels. But when David was writing, a person's name was more than a label. As a rule, today, names do not mean much at all. I believe that is one reason why being able to use the name of Jesus does not mean very much to many Christians.

God has given us a name to use that is above every other name, the name that He has exalted. When David was writing, they knew all the names for God. They knew, for example, that when they prayed to *El Shaddai*, they were saying "All-Sufficient One, You can supply everything we need."

The closest thing we have in our society to the use of names in the way the Israelites did is what we call "name dropping." If you want a special favor from those in authority, you can use some important person's name as if he were your personal friend. However, if that person really *is* your personal friend, you are careful not to abuse that friendship by throwing his or her name around loosely.

In those days, it was the same way. When you were in covenant with someone or had permission to use his name, all he was and all he had was at your disposal when you called on his name.

I understand that in some places in the Middle East until this day, the Arabs have continued this tradition. I heard this story several years ago:

An Arab named Aba Shosho lived in the desert close to a large oasis. He was very, very wealthy with enough men in his family along with servants to make up a small army to protect his holdings. One day another Arab was traveling across the desert not very far from this oasis, when a band of robbers began to chase him.

He did whatever you do to get a camel to run, but the robbers were getting closer and closer. So the man being chased headed straight for the oasis and began to call Aba Shosho's name.

Aba was sitting in his tent taking it easy, because it was during the heat of the day. He heard his name being called. Now, if he did not bother to go check out the situation, his name would be dishonored. A man in distress was calling his name. If he just sat on in the cool of his tent and ignored the call, he would bring dishonor on his name.

The word would get out that Aba Shosho will not back up his name. So he got up, called his little army to mount up, rode out on the desert, and rescued this guy. Then he brought the traveler to his tent, fed him, and gave him water. You might say that old Shosho "set him securely on high."

Also, as long as the traveler was in the tent, Aba Shosho's name was still on the line. So he posted his followers around the oasis to keep the robbers away. If they came any closer, his men would kill them if necessary. They would do what was necessary to see that this man who called upon the name of their lord was not harmed in any way.

The man could have stayed there as long as he wanted, because he called on Aba Shosho's name, and there is nothing in tradition that says, ''after thirty days, the use of the name runs out.''

You need to understand that, in even a greater way, God is going to see that the name of Jesus is never dishonored. If you call upon the Father in the name of Jesus, according to the Word of God, the Word will be fulfilled. Jesus has already done everything He can to bring that principle into reality in your life.

Jesus said:

> **Whatsoever ye shall ask the Father in my name, he will give it you.**
>
> **Hitherto have ye asked nothing in My name: ask, and ye shall receive, that your joy may be full.**
>
> **John 16:23b,24**

A lot of people have set their love upon God, and He has delivered them. They love God with all their hearts and their neighbors as themselves. But they have never been taught that they can use the name of Jesus. They do not know that, even now, they are sitting in heavenly places in Him. They do not know they can speak the Word of God in the name of Jesus and see the Word work in their lives.

Then there are others who have a hard time setting their love on God. Yet, when there is a disaster, a problem, or a situation in their lives, they call out and expect God to get them out of a mess. But when He does, they want to go on their way and still not set their love upon Him.

A Long Life

God said that if one who has his love set on God calls Him, He *will* answer and be with him in trouble. God said

He would deliver that one and honor him. If tradition shows us that earthly men honored their names to the extent revealed in Middle Eastern culture, then how much more must God honor the name of Jesus?

The last verse of that psalm is particularly encouraging.

With long life will I satisfy him, and shew him my salvation.

Second Kings, Chapter 20, records a very interesting story that I would like for us to consider. A man whose name was Hezekiah was very sick. In fact, the first verse of this chapter says that the prophet Isaiah came to him and told him that he was going to die.

I think that would be a difficult thing to deal with. It is bad enough to be informed by a physician that you don't have long to live. But to be told by a prophet that God says you are going to die is much worse. I think most people would just accept that word as being final.

Hezekiah did not. Verse 3 tells us that he prayed, **I beseech thee, O Lord, remember now how I have walked before thee in truth and with a perfect heart, and have done that which is good in thy sight. And Hezekiah wept sore.**

This man prayed the very best prayer he knew how to pray. God heard that prayer and sent Isaiah back to give Hezekiah an answer.

And it came to pass, afore Isaiah was gone out into the middle court, that the word of the Lord came to him, saying,

Turn again, and tell Hezekiah the captain of my people, Thus saith the Lord, the God of David thy father, I have heard thy prayer, I have seen thy tears: behold, I will heal thee: on the third day thou shalt go up unto the house of the Lord.

And I will add unto thy days fifteen years; and I will deliver thee and this city out of the hand of the

**king of Assyria; and I will defend this city for mine
own sake, and for my servant David's sake.**

**And Isaiah said, Take a lump of figs. And they
took and laid it on the boil, and he recovered.**

2 Kings 20:4-7

I must confess that I really do not know why God used
that lump of figs to restore this man's health. It really does
not matter. It worked! So let me come to the point of why
I chose to consider this story.

If God said to me, "I'm going to add fifteen years to
your life; beginning today, you have fifteen more years to
live," I would respond, "That is not enough."

Why would I say that? Simply because I am not sure
that in fifteen years I will be totally satisfied with life.

I am sure that someone will read this and be aghast
that I would make such a statement.

There is such a strong belief in the religious world that
"we have no promise of tomorrow," that my comments
seem ridiculous. But I believe that we do have a promise
of tomorrow.

Throughout this book I have been sharing with you
some very specific instructions for living a long life. I am
completely convinced that those who diligently and
faithfully do the things spoken of in the psalms are assured
of tomorrow. In fact, it is more than a promise. It is a
declaration that we can live until we are satisfied with life.

One could respond, "But you have not had a prophet
sent to you personally by God to tell you how much longer
you can live." My response is that I have no need of such
a messenger. I have God's Word.

I am doing my very best to convince you to accept and
believe the Bible in a very personal way. It is God talking
to you.

God wants you to live. God wants you to live a long, satisfying life. And, there is a very good reason why He wants that for you.

I believe that Jesus gave us some insight into this situation in what is recorded in John 15:16. Jesus said to His disciples, **Ye have not chosen me, but I have chosen you, and ordained you, that ye should go and bring forth fruit, and that your fruit should remain: that whatsoever ye shall ask of the Father in my name, he may give it you.**

God chose you. Through the Lord Jesus, He chose you to fulfill a purpose on this earth. Do not ever allow the devil to cause you to think otherwise. God has a reason for you to be alive.

What is that reason? So that you can bear fruit. I am talking about the fruit of the Spirit. God wants all nine of the fruit of the Spirit in full manifestation in your life. (Gal. 5:22,23.) God is not satisfied that your life is over until that fruit is manifested in your life. How much longer am I going to live? I can give you an idea of how much longer God wants you to live. He desires for all that fruit to be manifested in your life. But then He is not satisfied with that being the end of your life. He said that He wants your fruit to remain. What does that mean?

God desires that love, joy, peace, longsuffering, gentleness, goodness, faith, meekness, and temperance be so evident in your life that other people will want to know God because of knowing you. That is reason enough to go on living.

So I am going to live. God is not through with me yet.

Let's have the fruit growing, developing, manifesting in our lives. Let's begin to share that fruit with others. There are a lot of people who do not have love in their lives. There are a lot of people who do not have joy in their lives. There are a lot of people who do not have peace in their lives.

If you could share the peace of God with them, or His love or joy, it could completely change their lives. That is reason enough to go on living. I have not yet given God's love, joy and peace to enough people who desperately need it. So, I am not satisfied with life.

. . . with long life will I satisfy him. I want you to stop reading for a moment and say those words out loud. "With long life will I satisfy him." *God wants you to be satisfied with life.* So many people die (before they would naturally die of old age) because they are dissatisfied with life. I believe that is why they die — because of their dissatisfaction with life.

A little trouble kills a lot of people. Worry, anxiety, frustration, and fear often bring death. But according to Psalm 91:16, the only reason to die is because you are satisfied with life. Live until you are absolutely satisfied with living.

How long will that take? Personally, I do not think I am close enough to know. So I am going to go on living.

I know these are very simple English words, but I decided to check their meaning in Hebrew to see if it would add richness to their English meaning.

The Hebrew word translated *life* is from an unused root meaning "to *be hot; a day* (as the *warm* hours), whether lit. (from sunrise to sunset, or from one sunset to the next), or fig. (a space of time defined by an associated term). . .''[1]

The Hebrew word translated *satisfy* means "to sate, i.e. *fill* to satisfaction (lit. or fig.): — have enough. . .'' It can even mean to "be weary of.''[2]

---

[1]Strong, *Hebrew and Chaldee Dictionary*, p. 48, #3117.
[2]Strong, *Hebrew and Chaldee Dictionary*, p. 112, #7646.

I believe that God is saying to us, "You can have as many sunsets as it takes to satisfy you." I have not had enough yet.

You can have so many sunsets that are so satisfying that you grow weary from so much satisfaction.

How very far that is from the way most of the population of this earth is living. Why is it that way?

I sincerely believe I have given you many of the reasons in this book. Most of the world does not know God. And many of those who do know Him do not follow the very simple guidelines of this psalm. I believe that fact is determining both the level of satisfaction they find in life and how long they live.

What kind of life do you have? Is it satisfying? Or is it very troubled? Is your life rich and rewarding? Or would you really just as soon your life be over? Perhaps you are afraid for your life to end. You need not be.

It is no coincidence that this great psalm ends with the phrase . . . **and shew him my salvation** (v. 16).

The Hebrew word for *salvation* means *"deliverance;* hence *aid, victory, prosperity:* — . . . health, help, . . . save . . . "[3]

If your life is not a satisfying one, let me urge you to turn to Jesus. Let Him help you. Let Him bring victory and deliverance into your life. He longs to give you the aid you need, even financial and physical aid.

Look toward heaven right now and ask God to help you and to change your life.

You can pray a very simple prayer, something like this:

God, I need Your help. Life is not going well for me. In fact, I am hurting deep inside. I need You, God. I need You very much. Give to me the deliverance, the victory, You said You would show to those who would live according to the words of the psalm.

---

[3]*Strong, Hebrew and Chaldee Dictionary*, p. 53, #3444.

I have not lived by the words of this psalm. But today I am making the decision to do so, to the best of my ability. So I ask that You help me.

I choose right now to accept Jesus as my Savior. Lord, I choose to believe that You sent Him to this earth to die for me. I believe that You raised Him from the dead. And at this moment in my life, I am trusting in Jesus.

So thank You for hearing and answering my prayer. In Jesus' name I ask these things. Amen.

Your choice to believe what God has said in Psalm 91 is the deciding factor. If you believe what you just prayed, God will answer that prayer. God will show you His salvation.

Confess the following frequently:

Because I dwell in the secret place of the most High, I abide in the shadow of the Almighty, in the light of His glorious presence. I am a part of the family of God, those who are born again of His Spirit.

The Lord is my refuge and my fortress. He is my shelter and protection, my way of escape from all danger and harm. I walk in His Word, clothed in His armor. He is my rock and my fortress, my deliverer; my God, my strength, and my high tower.

He delivers me from all snares, traps, and temptation. In Him I turn away from evil and rise up over sin. He has given me power to tread on serpents and scorpions, and over all the power of the enemy.

My God covers me with His feathers, and in His wings I trust. He hedges me in so that the evil one cannot touch me. Because of my trust in Him, I walk boldly by faith so that I am not afraid of the terror at night, the pestilence in darkness or the destruction at noon. I fear no evil, but my reverent fear is in the Lord.

Because I choose to walk in faith and in love, no harm will come to me. A thousand may fall at my side, and ten thousand at my right hand, but it will not come near me. No weapon formed against me will prosper.

With my eyes I will behold the reward of the wicked, those who are terrified at night, hit by arrows, destroyed by pestilence, consumed by fear. Because I am a Christian, I do not expect the horrible things that happen to others to happen to me. Since I have made the Lord, the most High, my refuge and habitation, no evil will befall me, no plague will come near my dwelling.

The Lord has given His angels charge over me, to keep me in all my ways. They watch over me and act in my behalf, just as they watched over, guided and protected the children of Israel and the apostles. The angels of the Lord make up a hedge around me and my family. They bear me up in the palms of their hands.

Therefore I will tread on the lion and the adder, the young lion and the dragon will I trample under foot. As a joint heir with Christ Jesus, all things — including Satan, the roaring lion — are under my feet.

Because the Lord has set His love on me — and I have set mine on Him — He delivers me and sets me on high. I call upon Him and He answers me. Satan can no longer hold me hostage because I have been delivered from him and his power.

With long life the Lord satisfies me, and He shows me His salvation. Before the foundation of the world, He chose me and set me apart to fulfill His purpose on this earth. He has a reason for me to live and not die. I have no fear of my life ending prematurely for the Lord has saved me from sin, sickness, fear, poverty and death and has delivered me into righteousness, health, peace, prosperity and life in all its fullness, joy, satisfaction and abundance. Thanks be to God!

What an incredible psalm! I challenge you to live it every day of your life.

Dr. Kennith E. Stewart: Author, pastor, college professor, consultant to Bible schools, and traveling minister, is best known and loved for his straight forward teaching of the Word of God.

For many years the focus of Dr. Stewart's ministry has been family relationships. He has authored several books which deal with this vital area of life. He is in much demand as a speaker, traveling throughout this country and other countries of the world to minister the Word of God to families. His extensive knowledge of God's Word is always presented in profound, yet practical, truths which have helped many to have meaningful lives whether single or married.

Dr. Stewart attended Brite Divinity School, Texas Christian University, Forth Worth, Texas, where he received his Master of Divinity degree and his Doctor of Ministry degree.

He is the founder and Pastor of Family Worship Center in Tulsa, Oklahoma, where he resides with his wife Donna, and his two sons, Jonathan and Jason.

For a complete list of tapes and
books by Dr. Stewart, write:

Dr. Kennith Stewart
P. O. Box 2493
Broken Arrow, OK 74013-2493

*Please include your prayer requests
and comments when you write.*

Additional copies of this book
are available from your local bookstore
or from:

HARRISON HOUSE
P. O. Box 35035
Tulsa, Oklahoma 74153

In Canada contact:

Word Alive
P. O. Box 284
Niverville, Manitoba
CANADA R0A 1EO

For international sales in Europe,
contact:

Harrison House Europe
Belruptstrasse 42 A
A - 6900 Bregenz
AUSTRIA

The Harrison House Vision

Proclaiming the truth and the power
Of the Gospel of Jesus Christ
With excellence;

Challenging Christians to
Live victoriously,
Grow spiritually,
Know God intimately.